"*GOLF from Point A* is a new book that's worth the read for several reasons. The information in *GOLF from Point A* presents mental concepts that have already enhanced the golf games of both professional and club golfers, ones that will help every golfer who applies the concepts in the book.

Before we swing, it is what we do mentally; what we are thinking about and when we are thinking, that supports or suppresses our current golf skills during both play and practice. FACT!

GOLF from Point A provides a different and in my view, a more useful application and understanding of the well-known concept of "play one shot at a time," by having students mentally and physically always play *GOLF from Point A*. This concept, when put to use has been a game changer."

MICHAEL HEBRON
PGA Hall of Fame

"*Point A* is more than just a way to play golf it is a way life. I have not only improved my golf game but I have found much more clarity and joy on and off the course using the tools that Point A offers."

BRITTANY BENVENUTO
Symetra Tour, 2015 Symetra Rising Star Award

"Playing at *Point A* is a tremendous asset to have on the golf course. By being in the moment, not worrying about the past or the future, I am able to play with more freedom and to the best of my ability. This strategy has been my biggest tool while playing tournament golf."

JONATHON KHAN
Canadian Tour

"My son shared the philosophy of his *Point A* golf lessons with me. I love the idea of living in the moment and focusing on the things that you can control, rather than the things that you can't! I've found this to be very helpful in my business and life in general. Also, my son's golf game is improving nicely as he incorporates playing from *Point A* into his game."

LISA FRANK
President and CEO, The Lisa Frank Company

"*Point A* is about having the same process every time. At *Point A* you have the same thoughts each time, not caring where the ball goes and then reacting the same way every time. Accepting the shot for what it is, always being positive and reacting in a positive manner. *Point A* has allowed me to take a lot of the stress away. I have been 6 over after 5 holes and then shot even par the rest of the way because I stuck with *Point A*."

L.P.
High School Golf Team

"Now that I am aware of playing golf from *Point A* and staying in the moment, I am acutely aware of how my playing partners totally destroy their games with all of their negative talk and expectations. I hear them say, 'Well, this is going to be a double.' And sure enough it is. Or 'Oh no, I don't want to three putt like the last hole.' It becomes a self-fulfilling prophecy and they don't even see it!!"

B.S.
8 Handicap, age 74

"*Point A* allows me to not be so helter-skelter when I am on the golf course. I have a plan that I can fall back on and if I get off track I just go back to *Point A*. If I had a bad hole, I remind myself to be at *Point A*, it's like starting over again. I feel more in control of me."

R.E.
22 Handicap

"I played 9 holes with my son and neither of us kept score so we could be at *Point A* without concerning ourselves with our scores. We both relaxed and enjoyed golf more than ever. The concept of *Point A* is straightforward and it allows kids and grownups to move on, which is a blessing in life and in golf."

J.S.
27 Handicap

"I went out to play the other day with a new perspective after reading only a few chapters of *GOLF from POINT A*. My mind was clear and positive and the result was wonderful. I hit some great shots and some misses as well but I didn't dwell on them and I was able to return rather quickly to positive thoughts. I twice hit it into bunkers, which was never a happy place for me. Each time I had positive thoughts and the results left me with a big smile and my surprised playing partners asking, 'who was that?' I can't wait to finish reading the book. It is really changing my enjoyment of the game and my handicap as well."

L.S.
24 Handicap, age 82

GOLF
FROM POINT A

SUSIE MEYERS VALERIE LAZAR

Golf from *Point* A

For more limericks, see *Limericks We Lived* (2014) by B. T. Enos (ISBN 9788-1-304-73537-9)

Editors make a book appear as if it were effortless to write. Thank you to Brooke Payne and the staff at Jera Publishing for doing just that with their guidance, encouragement, and patience.

Jacket design: David Niles

ISBN 978-0-9972718-0-5 (hard cover)
ISBN 978-0-9972718-1-2 (paperback)

Published by: Point of View Productions, LLC.

Find the best of your game at *Point A*,

Aware it's the place you should stay.

Accept the shot dumb,

And allow what might come.

Simply be at *Point A* when you play.

—B.T. ENOS AND VALERIE LAZAR

PREFACE

A special thanks goes to my good friend and partner in this project, Valerie Lazar. She has been the catalyst and the reason this book is in print now. Her passion for golf and her desire to help others gave her the impetus to say, "Let's do something with these ideas, maybe a video or a book!" Her writing skills and remarkable insights to the process of creating this book have made it unique and interesting. Valerie brings a wonderful perspective to this book. She has great common sense and a way with words. Her tireless work and great wit have made this book stand on its own. She was determined not to make it a tutorial, a "how to" carbon copy of what is already on the market, and she has done a great job.

When I was an instructor in New York early in my career, Valerie took lessons from me. She was the club champion and a fine golfer. I left New York to teach in Miami and Dallas and eventually landed in Tucson, Arizona. It was years before we met up again as I was busy teaching and raising two children. Valerie came out to Arizona to work on her game with me and experienced a big difference in the way I taught. She noticed she was improving because her thoughts were changing. She was experiencing a new method of learning. She had not heard concepts like these before and was very excited about getting these ideas out to the public so more people could find a joyful approach to improving their game.

Through hours of churning and honing these concepts over the years and with her creative writing, we now have *Golf from Point A*. Our hope is that you will find some useful insights that give you the power to do what you want to do and be who you want to be on the golf course.

SUSIE MEYERS

CONTENTS

INTRODUCTION

Let's get right to the point. Everyone falls in love with golf the same way. The moment you experience the exhilaration of sending a golf ball soaring into the air, you want to do it again and again and make it go farther each time. As soon as you've holed your first bogey, par, or birdie putt, you want to hear that wonderful kerplunkity, gurgily sound again. Every time you post a new low score, you set your sights on shooting a lower one.

From that first glorious airborne beauty, it's love at first flight. You're hooked on the game, and like every other golfer out there, you want to play better. From beginners to PGA professionals, everyone is always looking to improve something about their stroke or their game, and a big part of the allure of the game is that everyone can. How to improve is the question, and the straightforward *Point A* approach to learning about *you* and what the driving force behind an effortless and effective golf stroke just might be the answer.

Mastering the technique that produces the perfect golf swing isn't the whole game, not by a long shot. The longest hitter doesn't always come out on top. A beautiful swing won't get you around the golf course or your name engraved on a trophy either. Because technique is only a part of making an effective shot, superior skills are wasted on the golfer who can't rely on them. If you're expecting to read detailed studies about how the brain works, the latest technical data about the golf swing, or where your body is supposed to be in any given millisecond of the swing, close the cover and put this book down. You won't find any of that here. What you will find is the Marvelous You and the door to the Marvelous Golfer you can become with *Point A* golf.

Point A offers a system that uses simple concepts to produce big results. Help yourself to any one of the ideas in *Point A* thinking, and you'll see how easily a *Point A* point of view can help you play better golf and get more enjoyment out of playing. Because golf is as much an art as it is a science, there's no right or wrong way to do it and no need to fit into any idealized notion of the perfect anything. The game is meant to be played differently by each individual because every shot is as unique as the golfer who creates it.

Point A is a concept and a process for improving your golf by changing how you think about yourself and the game. It's a starting point, a turning point, and a point of no return all in one. From novice to professional, *Point A* thinking is a system that offers the clarity and direction that's needed to develop a reliable thought process that is the foundation of a strong golf game.

You can think about the past and worry about something that's over and done, but there's nothing you can do to change it. You can think about the future and imagine outcomes that cause you to feel anxious and fearful, but you can't make the future happen. You can't actually do anything at all in the past or the future. You can only physically be where you are now, in the present, and where you are now is *Point A*. Golf is played in the present!

With *Point A* thinking, you turn on your awareness and clear away the distracting clutter in your mind. You free yourself from the burden of *trying* so you can allow the club to swing with freedom. You accept where the ball will land before you make your stroke.

It doesn't matter if it's the first shot of the round, a lob shot floating over a bunker, or your last putt to break a previous low score, every shot is played from *Point A*. *Point A* thinking replaces copious notes and long to-do lists with a solid and reliable format for how to think, what to think, and when to think it. Golf can be as simple as that or as difficult as you want to make it.

Whether your dream is to be on top of your game or on the top of a leaderboard, *Point A* shows you how changing your point of view—which is infinitely easier and less time-consuming than changing the mechanics of your golf stroke—can improve everything about your game. *Point A* golf gives you the tools, the plan, and the path to a point of view that positively changes your mind, your stroke, and your game. And that's the point!

CHAPTER ONE

WHAT'S THE POINT?

THE SECRET

Many golfers seem to be on a lifelong quest to find the "secret" to shooting lower scores and owning a repeatable, reliable swing. If you're among them and, despite the library you've amassed, videos you've watched, tips you've tried, and lessons you've taken, you're still looking for golf's mysterious and elusive secret, your search is finally over. The secret is there is no secret.

It's true. There is no hidden secret, and no one believes it. Not you or anyone else. Secret or no secret, are you still holding fast to the dream that there must be something somewhere that can open the door to playing your best golf and enjoying every aspect of the game? If so, you're not alone and you're right, because there is something that can change everything—and it's not a secret at all. It's called *Point A* golf, a plan for learning and playing the game that's filled with so much common sense it makes you wonder why you haven't already thought of it.

Hiding in plain sight is the notion that the game itself ought to be what it originally was: a pleasant walk in the countryside carrying odd little sticks designed to advance a golf ball over hill and dale while also enjoying good company or welcome solitude. *Point A* thinking brings you to that marvelous and joyful game.

Whether you're an amateur or a professional, your point of view about the game and what it offers you is the starting point for how you play. Perhaps even more so in tournament conditions, playing your best is all about keeping the game simple, and that's exactly what *Point A* offers you.

SIMPLE OR COMPLEX?

Golf is a game of apparent simplicity and inherent complexity. At the time this book was written, "information about playing golf" typed into Google's Internet search engine yielded 258,000,000 results, a mind-boggling amount of information about a game. Searching the term "information about rocket science" returned an underwhelming 4,060,000—an astonishingly fewer number of results on a subject that's far more complex. How can this ancient game that's played with a variety of clubs and a very small dimpled ball in a large open field be so much more complicated than rocket science? It defies belief.

The number of volumes dedicated to golf that are already in print would lead you to surmise that the game requires intense study, but golf can actually be one of the simplest games to play. The ball is just sitting there. You're not forced to block it, return it, or run anywhere with it. You decide where you want it to go and when to hit it, and no one interferes with your stroke once you begin to make it. It sounds like little could go wrong, and yet it does.

Why every shot isn't perfect is a question that doesn't require a library of golf books to answer. The essence of making golf strokes and playing the game boils down to one basic truth: your thoughts before a shot, after a shot, and in between shots will have a greater effect on every aspect of your game than mastering all the conflicting theories on the best technique for swinging a golf club.

PGA Tour player Michael Thompson, winner of the 2013 Honda Classic, was asked in a post-win interview to share his most important thought about playing competitive golf:

> THE CHALLENGE IS KEEPING IT SIMPLE.
> SIMPLE IS PLAYING FROM POINT A.
>
> —Michael Thompson

If keeping your thoughts simple is the challenge, how does playing from *Point A* prepare golfers—from beginners to PGA Tour winners—to meet and conquer that challenge? How you play is directly influenced by your point of view, so first look within yourself to see exactly what *you* bring to the game when you play. Golf will be what you perceive it to be: simple or complex, fun or frustrating, challenging or impossible. Simple is easier, usually more efficient, and much more fun. The best of the very best in the world are able to play at their very best when they keep it simple, and you can choose to do that too. *Point A* shows you how.

I HEAR A VOICE

Of course you hear a voice. Everyone does. It's the soundtrack of your every thought that talks to you throughout the round. In fact, playing golf or not, you hear it all the time. It's very busy telling you what it wants you to do, often impatiently interrupting, disrupting, and disputing whatever thoughts you already have in mind.

It can be your best friend or your worst enemy. It can build you up or tear you down. It can tell you the truth or a lie. It can be your coach, your mentor, and your in-house cheerleader all wrapped up in one. It can also be the voice of all your insecurities and fears and lead you straight to your downfall. The voice can simplify or complicate everything, so it's definitely in your best interest to take charge of what it says!

Whether it's for money, medals, or the pure joy of playing the game, when you don't control your thoughts, you undermine your chances to play to your potential. It doesn't matter if it's a two-dollar Nassau, the club championship, the U.S. Open, or a casual round with your friends, how you manage you and how you choose to think has more influence on your stroke and your scores than having a technically perfect swing.

It's the voice in your head and not the wedge in your hand that turns a chip into a chunk. What you tell yourself can sabotage the shot or give you the confidence to just do it. You are 100 percent in charge of what you think while you play.

THINK ABOUT IT . . .

Point A golf doesn't put the spotlight on statistics compiled by a computer that collates information about how often the ball lands where it does because of your launch angle and attack angle. "What you think" rather than "how you swing" is the focus of *Point A* thinking. Despite all the modern technological advances that have given golfers the means to analyze every swing path, how much the ball spins, how far it rolls, and when a specific body part moves—the average handicap of the American golfer

(16.1 for men and 29.2 for women) hasn't changed significantly over the last thirty years.

Although the data that's gathered by the newest state-of-the-art equipment is intellectually enticing to contemplate and tempting to try to incorporate into your stroke, do you really need (or even want) to be concerned about all these details? Does it matter whether or not the numbers on the machines are as good as they could be (whatever that means) when your only true desire is simply to get the ball to go where you want it to?

You can find and fine-tune the game you're looking for in your head well before it reaches the club in your hands. Your natural physical abilities will certainly factor into the skill level you're able to achieve and maintain, but it's clear that spending the majority of the time you allot to the game practicing the technique of your golf stroke on the range isn't the only thing you'll need to reach your potential.

> COMPETITIVE GOLF IS PLAYED MAINLY
> ON A FIVE-AND-A-HALF-INCH COURSE,
> THE SPACE BETWEEN YOUR EARS.
>
> —Bobby Jones

Bobby Jones, one of the greatest players of all time, knew it. Jordan Spieth, credited with having one of the strongest mental games in the history of golf, knows it. In fact, most professionals, low-handicap amateurs, and enlightened players with midrange handicaps know it too. When a tournament leader loses a two-shot lead with a hook out of bounds on the final tee of a four-day championship, it isn't because of a forgotten technical move in the golf stroke.

Every touring professional agrees there is a great deal more to the game than the machine-like perfection it requires to drive the ball 325 yards down the middle of the fairway. They know that capitalizing on that skill requires having more than the skill itself. The unseen dimension that leads to more successful shots more often is clear and positive thinking *before* the stroke is made. Believing you can do it is often more important than knowing exactly how you're able to do it.

Have you ever missed a shot and said, "I just knew I was going to miss it"? How did you know? What were you thinking before you made your stroke? Were you waffling back and forth between choices, uncertain about exactly which shot you wanted to make or which club to use, not really committing to any of them? It's actually quite simple: If you think you can't make a shot, you won't. If you think you can, the odds are more in your favor to succeed. Your best swing is more about trust than torque.

Everyone of any age and any size can improve. Anyone—from beginners to scratch golfers—can increase the joy of playing by building up their confidence instead of their libraries. Exactly what is confidence and what makes it grow? Confidence is a state of mind, and that's the whole point: Everything you think before a stroke has an effect on every shot you make.

GOLF IS 95% MENTAL
…AND THE OTHER 5% IS MENTAL.

—Anonymous

Will a lack of commitment to your shot or club selection chip away at your confidence and cause you to make a stroke that can't possibly deliver the desired outcome? You bet! It happens more often than not to you and everyone else. Your mind is the command post for how you'll play. Once you're aware of what thoughts you have in your mind before you plan a shot or make a stroke, you can learn to reroute or, even better, not even entertain ideas that cause feelings of regret or fear.

YOUR THOUGHTS CONTROL EVERYTHING

Improving your golf game is more about where your mind is than where your backswing is. Like looking for love in all the wrong places, looking for the perfect swing is the wrong place to find your game. The right place to look is within *you*, where you'll discover who you are, how you operate, and how you learn. Take a look at what you think and when you think, and you'll soon realize your thoughts affect everything in your golf stroke: your timing, your tempo, and your turn. You control your thoughts, and your thoughts control everything.

Why do you miss the 7-iron shot on the course that you hit perfectly ten times when you warmed up on the range? After three drives straight down the middle of the fairway, why does the next one hook into the trees or barely make it off the tee? It's all about what *you* are thinking.

Do you seem to lose your swing someplace between the range and the course? Do you then spend the rest of your round looking for it or fixing it? The truth is that it isn't lost at all. It's just temporarily missing during the action of your golf stroke. When your practice-range swing becomes one you don't even recognize on the course, something actually did change. *You* changed. The malfunction that suddenly appeared in your technique began with the thoughts you had *before* the swing was set in motion.

Many golfers unknowingly morph from not caring very much about where the ball goes during practice at the range to caring too much about where it goes on the course. Does the same thing happen to you? You couldn't have forgotten so quickly how to make the strokes you just practiced. It's the same *you* hitting the same shots you know how to hit, but on the course, you're not getting the same results. What happened to *you* and how did it show up in your golf stroke?

Simply put, trying trumped trust. The carefree swing you had on the range collapsed under the weight of suddenly wanting very specific results. You changed your intention from patiently waiting for a desired result from a particular stroke to feeling the pressure of wanting a shot that fulfills an expectation.

YOU CONTROL YOUR THOUGHTS

Negative thoughts take you far away from where you should be: in the present preparing for your next shot. You can't focus on the shot at hand when you're too pre-occupied with finding something—anything—that will save you when waves of fear and doubt engulf you in despair. You're busy looking for a rope that can either rescue you from the riptide or use to hang yourself with.

The frustration of it all leads many an exasperated golfer to blurt out, "I've had it! I'm quitting this game!" They never mean it, and when you say it, neither do you. You calm down and hope you will figure out something new to try before your next round that will put an end to your golf miseries instead of your golf career.

On the course, have you ever:
* projected an embarrassingly high score early in the round because of a few errant shots and then lost interest in playing?
* been unable to sink the short putts that you didn't miss on the practice green?

* worried about where the ball would go?
* been angry about the lie of the ball?
* wasted time dwelling on the putt you just missed?
* called yourself an idiot...or much worse?

Will going back to the range immediately after the round to prove to yourself that you can do it give you what you need? Hitting buckets of 7-iron shots and fifty drives in a row to fix the problem won't necessarily make a big difference in your game because that doesn't address what really went wrong for you on the course.

You'll get far better results from getting a grip on the kinds of thoughts that caused you and your game to sink on the course. Ask, "What was I thinking on the course before my shots?" and your answers will give you some insight into the high correlation between good thoughts and good shots. "Was I positive or negative?" "Was I confident or doubtful?" After the voice said, "I'm not sure this is the right club," "You stink," or "What if I don't get out of this bunker?" were you still able to make a great shot?

If you want to know how to prevent future fainting spells on the course, begin with becoming aware of the thoughts that interfere with your golf stroke when your game begins to unravel. Before they even have a chance to get into your head, replace those thoughts with ideas that work for you instead of against you.

Are you having an "Aha!" moment as you see the mind–body connection in your own past failures and successes? Whatever plays out between your ears will govern the game you play on the course. Assess your approach to the game and allow *Point A* thinking to change your mind to positively change your game.

CHAPTER TWO

YOUR POINT OF VIEW

A PLACE IN TIME

Point A is a place in time—this moment right now and right here. *Point A* is where the ball is and where the player should be. As absurd as it may sound, too many golfers are someplace else. They might be in the past, struggling to fix a swing flaw they diagnosed after the last missed shot. They might be in the future, with worries of an imagined disaster that's yet to occur. In either case, those golfers simply aren't here at *Point A*, in the present, preparing to make this shot.

When you're busy regretting the last shot that didn't go where you wanted it to, you're putting energy into going nowhere. Ruminating about possible outcomes, like "What if I hit it in the water or leave it short?" won't point you in a helpful direction either. You want to be at *Point A*, in the present, with a calm and uncluttered mind that will allow you to make the same free and fluid strokes on the course that you make with ease at the driving range. There's no reason to love or hate the ball because of where it is or dwell on the story of how it got there. It really doesn't matter. It is where it is—the only place it can be: at *Point A*.

It doesn't matter
    if it was your best shot ever or your worst miss.
What does matter
    is your preparation for the next shot.

It doesn't matter
    if it's in the middle of the fairway or behind a tree.
What does matter
    is your reaction to where it is.

It doesn't matter
    if it's where you intended the ball to land or not.
What does matter
    is what you do now.

The shot you make from where the ball is now, here at *Point A*, is the only shot that ever matters. That's why it deserves 100 percent of your attention and ability. When the shot is over, it's over. Follow the ball to *Point A* and begin the process again. No pouting about the past, no predictions for an outcome in the future, just playing from *Point A*.

A BIRDIE PUTT EQUALS A WHIFF?

Scorecard math is very straightforward: a number is a number is a number. The numbers on your scorecard represent every shot you make during the round. There may be sensational stories to tell about some of them, but on the card, they are only numbers. Golfers who have already figured this out know when they pay equal attention to every shot; the payoff is lower scores.

All golf shots are not the same in the air or on the ground, but the chip-in from the rough, the punch shot from under the tree, and the forty-foot downhill slider into the cup for a par are all identical on the scorecard. There are no pictures of your two-hundred-and-fifty-yard drive, the sandy, the chunked chip, the birdie putt, or the whiff. There are only numbers. That's why at *Point A*, each shot is equal to every other shot *before* it becomes a number, which is what makes every shot on the course an equal opportunity for you to make the best stroke possible at that time from that place.

A putt is a putt is a putt. There are no birdie, bogey, or winning putts at *Point A*; there are only putting strokes. When you think of a putt as a birdie, par, or save-bogey putt, you increase its value to you and pile on the pressure. Making the putt becomes more important than making the stroke that will get the job done. The adrenaline of "do it or face the consequences" may boost some golfers' abilities, but for most, it only heightens their fear of failure.

Pondering the possible negative outcomes of a shot instead of preparing a plan for it takes you away from where you are, here at *Point A*, and propels you into an imagined scenario somewhere else. That vision can frighten you and unleash some intense emotions that will alter how your body moves. The shot is no longer equal to every other shot, even though it will still be one stroke, just like every other shot on your scorecard. Your mental trip into the future brings worries and burdens to the shot you have to make here and now, in the present. The anxiety you've created makes it all the more difficult for you to execute the shot to the best of your ability.

For some golfers, that's more than enough anxiety to suddenly turn a smooth putting stroke into a jab that sends the ball miles past the hole or leaves it pathetically short. Because the results of the shot have become more important than making the stroke for the shot, your focus leaves *Point A* and takes your best chance of making your best stroke with it.

CONNECT-THE-DOTS ... OR NOT?

Does your vision of how you'll play a particular hole resemble a connect-the-dots drawing? If it does, you're like millions of other golfers who stand on each tee and decide shot by shot how they plan to play the hole. Perhaps you even tie your shots together—Point A to Point B to Point C—from the tee all the way into the hole or connect each one to the next and the next until the final putt is made.

You tee it up with the hope that the ball will cooperate with your intended connect-the-shots plan, but because this is golf we're talking about, it goes astray and into the rough, behind a tree, or into the bunker. Now all the other shots you've strung together in your plan become useless. You're not where you think you are supposed to be and panic sets in.

You analyze what you believe was the broken golf stroke that sent the ball into never-never land and attempt to diagnose the cause of the problem so you can repair what went wrong before you have to make your next shot. You go through your mental Rolodex, looking for every fix you've ever heard of or read about. Now you're really confused and distraught.

You feel frustrated and maybe even downright disheartened as you huff and puff your way to the bunker. Long before you even get there, you begin to worry about the results of the bunker shot you haven't made yet. In desperation, you replay the how-to video "Blasting out of

Bunkers" in your mind. If you don't have much confidence in your bunker play, the situation becomes even more complicated. You begin thinking about an unwanted outcome in the future, which only makes you feel more and more anxious about how you're going to deal with making the shot here, in the present. It wasn't what you expected and suddenly you find that your game is coming apart at the seams.

You arrive at the bunker only to find the ball—and your hopes of getting out in one stroke—buried in the sand. This troubling sight triggers a cascade of negative emotions that wreak havoc within you as you twist and dig your feet into position. The bunker shot has just acquired some heavy baggage filled with disappointment and anxiety. Your fruitless analysis of the last shot and apprehension about making the next one weigh you down. All these concerns make you feel even more fearful and soon you're silently wondering why you even play this game and wishing there was some place to hide.

What you need to do now is change your point of view so you can get back on course mentally and physically. Return to *Point A* and see the bunker shot as the fresh start it really is. Leave the past behind, expect nothing from the future, and put your energy into doing your best from where the ball is now.

Don't be like the many golfers who pressure themselves right out of making a putt or a particular shot or shooting a good score by thinking about the possible results before the stroke even begins. Stay at *Point A,* where you can keep it simple, keep it equal, and keep yourself where the ball is—hitting more good shots more often and saving yourself a lot of unnecessary heartache.

> Zena was a new *Point A* student. Although it seemed a radical departure from adding up her score each step of the way, the idea of seeing each shot as its own entity did make a great deal of sense to her. Her *Point A* coach suggested they play nine holes together and see what happens.
>
> On the course, Zena easily adapted to having a positive outlook and staying in the present. She felt relieved and empowered to experience the freedom of not worrying about results before they happened. Her shot on the 125-yard par-3 landed five feet below the flagstick. On the green, she studied the line and, with newly discovered confidence, deftly drilled the ball into the cup! Her reaction was *Point A* perfect. She smiled and calmly announced, "This is my first birdie. I've had many opportunities before, but somehow my hands were always shaking and I missed every one. This time, I wasn't trying for a 'birdie two' on the hole. I told myself I was at *Point A*, and I made the same solid stroke I'd been making all day. And it worked!"

You can eliminate toting around what feels like the weight of the world from shot to shot if you don't connect your shots to each other. That's right, you want to dis-connect your shots. Why link your shots together anyway? They have nothing in common. Every shot calls for a different club, distance, and trajectory, and every shot is a singular event that will never happen exactly the same way again. Golf shots can't fall into a neat pattern because each one is separate and unique. Leave the memory in the past and move on to *Point A*, where the shot that deserves 100 percent of your attention is waiting for you.

THE GOLF BALL AT POINT A

A golf ball is a passionless, brainless, dimpled sphere of rubber that doesn't know where it is, where it's been, or where you think it's supposed to go next. It can't feel your pain or your joy about where it is as it sits motionless in the fairway, the bunker, or behind a tree. However, and refreshingly so, it really doesn't matter where the ball is physically when you perceive it to simply be at *Point A*. Only then, without any negative emotions attached to where the ball is, are you free to focus on the shot at hand—the *only* shot that matters—and do your best with it.

If you aren't a believer in *Point A* thinking yet, consider that when you throw a handful of balls into tough lies in the practice area so you can figure out how to play them, you actually enjoy the challenge and excitement of successfully making those difficult shots. You're not wasting time and energy on negative thoughts like bad break, bad lie, or bad luck; you're stimulated by the challenge. The next time you have an opportunity to create a shot on the course, remember the positivity you felt when you were experimenting with all those shots you've already practiced and proven you could make.

Playing from *Point A* feels exactly the same way. It offers the opportunity to create a shot that matches the situation at hand without any negative emotions interrupting your natural swing movement. Feelings of frustration because the ball is in a difficult lie are replaced with a positive outlook that allows you to become creative with your game and make awesome shots from awful places.

POINT A TO POINT A TO POINT A

Playing *Point A* golf is a process in itself. With *Point A* thinking, there are no evaluations or negative appraisals about where the ball lands. Look at your target, select your club, make your golf stroke, and then, without any comments, just notice where the ball lands: long or short, left or right. Nothing more. No judgements about what you didn't do or what you think you did wrong. The ball is where it is and nothing can change that. You simply play from *Point A* to *Point A* to *Point A*, repeating the same positive process over and over, shot after shot, until the last putt drops in the cup on the final hole.

At *Point A*, you're not "trying" to get the ball to go to "Point B." There is no "Point B." At *Point A*, you stand behind the ball, look at the target, and gather the information you need. You make your decision about the shot you want to make and continue to look at your target while you set up to the ball. Without confusion, doubt, or fear, the ball will most likely go somewhere near your target. Wherever it is, it will be at *Point A*. Beginners look at the flagstick, and the ball goes in that general direction. The expert player looks at the flagstick, and the ball snuggles right up to the hole. To the best of your ability, the ball will go where your eyes go.

With your focus directed solely on this shot and nothing else, you're able to make your best stroke possible in this moment from this place called *Point A*. Keep it simple. Don't overthink it. Look where you want the ball to go, and then allow yourself to make the appropriate stroke for the shot you created in your mind's eye.

Perhaps you believe that playing golf from *Point A* and just looking where you want the ball to go isn't enough—it's way too simple to work for you. If so, just watch any golf tournament on TV and count how many times tour players look at their target before they begin their golf stroke. You just might change your mind.

In the post-round interview of a player who just shot a remarkable low number, maybe 58 or 59, the onsite TV commentator asks the newly renowned player what swing thought was behind the extraordinary score. Viewers at home lean forward in their chairs, eagerly anticipating the secret that will be shared coast to coast and surely help everyone watching to play better the next time they're on the course. No matter who the professional is, the answer always seems to be the same: "I was just playing one shot at a time. I wasn't thinking anything."

It sounds easy enough—"one shot at a time"—but what they never seem to mention is how they do it. How do you play one shot at a time? And what about "I wasn't thinking anything"? What does that mean? The reality is the tour player truly wasn't thinking anything, which is to say he was not thinking anything that would distract him or bring him out of the zone.

But how do professionals get into that zone and stay there and, more importantly, can you? It's as easy as one, two, three. Begin with first clearing your mind of the "what ifs" and any muddy confusion over what shot you want to make. Second, don't waffle over which club to use, and third, *don't* put on the proverbial thinking cap laden with information and instructions before every shot; take it off. Intend to play with a quiet mind from *Point A* to *Point A* to *Point A*.

Some of the most impossibly difficult shots in golf have given the game some of its most memorable moments.

They occur so often that these incredible recovery shots from some of the most unlikely spots on the golf course aren't just lucky answers to their ill-fated predecessors; they are bona fide great shots made by great golfers who remained calm and unflustered by where the ball was.

Victor Dubuisson made two of the greatest up and downs in match play history during the 2014 Accenture Match Play Championship. On the 19th hole, with only the briefest deliberation, he hit a shot from a nearly impossible lie under a prickly bush onto the green and made the par putt to halve the hole. On the 20th hole—also from what appeared to be an all but impossible shot from the waste area where the ball was engulfed by a bush—once again, with very little time in the huddle, he made a routine (for him) shot that miraculously landed on the green and holed the putt.

There was no visible tension in either of the strokes he made from those challenging lies and no visible clue that missing either shot would cost him the tournament. Instead, the millions of spellbound viewers saw a golfer assess the situation, calmly create the shot he needed, and simply do it.

It appeared that he was able to play each of these spectacular shots from "bad luck" lies just like every other shot in the round. He was able to shrug off the shrubbery situations and concern himself with the shot at hand, not the ones that put him in the bushes or that might not get him out of trouble and lose the tournament for him. He seemed to play each shot from *Point A* without emotional interference from regretting how he got there or fears about where the ball would go next.

Can you learn to think this way? Absolutely. *Point A* is where nothing can hamper your thinking or your golf stroke. Playing from *Point A* to *Point A* helps you train yourself to calmly follow your routine no matter what happens, because the reality is, you can't control the situation you can only control your reaction to it and your preparation for the next shot.

PLAYING FROM POINT A

Point A prepares you to be able to treat each shot as the separate and unique entity that it is. The plan of action at *Point A* is three simple steps:

1. Make a clear decision about the shot.
   Select your club, based on the conditions: the lie, distance, wind, etc.

2. Visualize the shot.
   See the trajectory and where the ball will land. Trust that you can do it.

3. Make a golf stroke that matches your picture.
   Commit to your plan, accepting that the ball will land at *Point A*.

If you have a gut instinct about a shot, don't second-guess it. Make it part of your plan. Wavering between which shot and which club and how far only creates confusion about your intentions. The slightest indecision will undermine your confidence about the shot and affect your ability to make the stroke you envision, so if something "feels" right, go with it.

During your next round, notice what thoughts you had before your shots. Were you present and attentive to each shot? Compare your thoughts to the *Point A* checklist below to see what you might want to address and adjust.

You're not playing golf from *Point A* when you are:
* Analyzing your swing to fix it before your next shot.
* Playing the 10th hole while you're still upset about a missed shot on the 4th hole.
* Thinking, "I need to par the last three holes to shoot my career round."

You are not at *Point A* if you're like Dustin Johnson, lining up your eagle putt on the last hole of the 2015 U.S. Open, and you tell your caddie that having a one- putt to win the tournament is a dream come true. It's quite possible that with this vision of putting to win before he actually did or didn't win, Dustin's look into the future took his focus away from the present and perhaps the very process that had worked so well for the previous seventy-one holes.

One putt would have won it outright. Two putts would have forced an eighteen-hole playoff the next day. His three-putt finish drew gasps of disbelief, shock, and horror from the gallery as he suddenly fell into a tie for second.

You are playing golf from *Point A*:
* When you are in the present.
* When you have a positive outlook.
* When you are emotionally detached from the results.

You are at *Point A* if you're like Jordan Spieth, playing in the 2015 U.S. Open. After you lose the two-stroke lead you got by making birdie on the 16th hole with a double bogey on the 17th, you follow it up on the next hole by staying with the same process that got the birdie. You pay no attention to the bad luck that was part of the double and move on to the 18th hole. You know recovery is more valuable than remorse and move on. You stay in the present following your plan, and your *present* is the tap-in birdie on the final hole that becomes the stroke that wins the tournament.

NEW SWING OR NEW POINT OF VIEW?

Ryan is a young man whose livelihood is playing golf. He was raised in a small town where he learned the game without much formal instruction. He went to college, turned pro after graduating, and was a promising player on the mini tours. He'd had moderate success as a professional and was working his way to the PGA Tour when he decided he needed to improve his game in order to achieve his goal.

He went to a top golf instructor who told Ryan he would get him on the PGA Tour if Ryan just changed a few parts of his swing. The changes didn't help, so he went to another and another and yet another teacher, looking for the answer to why he couldn't take his game to the next level. With each instructor, his swing was repeatedly analyzed and dissected.

Long days were spent practicing the changes. Hitting golf balls for six or more hours a day was not unusual. Ryan believed if he worked hard enough and changed his swing to make it technically sound, surely his dream of playing on the PGA Tour would be fulfilled. But it wasn't. Disappointed but still hoping to improve his level of play, Ryan decided that playing golf from *Point A* was his next step. He tells his story this way:

> I see my game differently now. I used to search for the right moves in my stroke but now I don't think about how to make my stroke anymore. I play from *Point A* to *Point A* to *Point A* where I feel that every shot is a new beginning.

After every round of golf I look to see what needs work and I spend time on that. I don't stand on the practice tee for hours anymore and I rarely look at my swing on video. I realized I already had the skills but I didn't know I had them because I was so busy trying to perfect something that can't be perfected. Instead of worrying about my golf swing I just hit different kinds of shots and noticed how the flight of the golf ball matched the picture in my mind's eye.

Now I feel solid, positive, and prepared with a process for my next round. Somehow the lower scores seem to be happening with half the effort even though I'm not trying to shoot a low number. I rely on the mental process that I am working on that day and attempt to do the same process on every shot. I am having fun just playing golf.

At the end of the day I happily go home and spend time with my kids. Because I feel satisfied and confident I can leave my golf game at the course and enjoy my family. They've noticed a big difference in my attitude since I've stopped searching for perfection. My acceptance of the things I can't control has given me a feeling of inner calm that allows me to approach each shot with more confidence.

EXPECT THE UNEXPECTED

A huge part of the appeal and pure fun of playing golf is the unpredictable nature of the game and the element of surprise that's built into every shot. From the takeaway to the final roll of the ball somewhere on the course, where it stops, nobody knows! What you'll shoot for eighteen holes or what different shots will make up your score remains a mystery until the round is over.

Before you make your golf stroke, do you know exactly where the golf ball will land? You know you don't. Can you make the ball go where you intend to every time you make a golf shot? You know you can't. No one can. That's why every shot is a surprise. When you embrace that idea, you'll be well on your way to staying more levelheaded more often in your game.

The challenge never ends. Can I really pull this shot off? Can I chip it close enough for a tap-in par? Can I hit it high enough to clear this tree? Can I sink this putt from way back here? The unexpected can be disappointing or delightful, distracting or ducky, devastating or divine. Don't be surprised when the ball goes where you want it to, and don't be destroyed when it doesn't. Wherever it is, the ball is always at *Point A*. *Point A* thinking guarantees that you'll be there with it.

CHAPTER THREE

THE STARTING POINT

BRAIN POWER

Every golfer knows the undeniable value of making a golf stroke that's as impervious to breaking down under pressure as possible, but very few know where to find it. Look beyond slow-motion videos that can be stopped at any millisecond in the swing to see what the real power behind a solid golf stroke is.

Golfers reach plateaus where, try as they may, gathering more technical information doesn't shave a stroke off their scores. At every skill level of the game, golfers come to the realization that a swing in all the right positions at all the right moments isn't enough.

What causes a golfer, who needs a par on the 18th hole for a two-buck win from his pals, to deftly power his favorite fifty-yard pitch over the green as if it were shot from a cannon? What really causes this same golfer to then guarantee the loss of the hole with a three-putt? Did he suddenly forget how to chip or putt? Of course he didn't.

No matter how many years you've been playing or how skilled you are, there's just no technical explanation for the sudden appearance of a shank, slice, hook, or chunk. Let's face it: right elbow tucked in or not, on plane or off, doing it "right" doesn't guarantee a successful stroke.

Golf would be predictable and boring if all one needed to excel at the game was the ability to repeat the exact swing and hit the exact same shots on demand. Iron Byron, the USGA ball-hitting robot can do it, humans can't. Like the Scarecrow in *The Wizard of Oz*, the robot with the picture-perfect swing needs a brain that can factor in the desire to succeed, the lie, the distance, the wind, and the appropriate club selection for the shot in order to be a real live golfer. Exploring the role your brain plays in your game is fascinating, but thankfully, you don't need a degree in neurology to play well or thoroughly enjoy the game.

Your point of view is the force behind both the unforgettably magnificent shot and the one that didn't wind up anywhere near where you intended it to go. Think with fear and you get a fearfully awful result. Think with confidence and every part of you teams up to make what you envision simply happen. When you know how to train your brain to work for you, you can change your stroke, your strategy, and your scores.

THINKING AND DOING

If entry into this world included an instruction manual detailing how the human body works, the neurology chapter would have a section on the two separate and extremely smart operation centers in the brain that control thinking and doing. Some scientists refer to these functions of the brain as the thinking and doing brains or the modern and reptilian brains. Others refer to them as the conscious and subconscious brains. Whichever nomenclature you prefer, the functions are the same. You are both a thinker and a doer, and the mental game of golf is about controlling your thinking to get the most out of what you're doing. It's that simple.

You began developing your thinking brain well before you uttered your first word, and the more you studied throughout your life, the more you learned. The thinking brain is where ideas are born, decisions are made, and problems are solved.

The doing brain controls motor skills, like walking, throwing a ball, and making a golf stroke. The doing brain learns how to do these things from making mistakes, trial and error, and repetition. The doing brain reacts to pictures in your mind, your senses, and your emotions—not to words. Your thoughts and words turn into pictures. When you play golf, the clearer and more positive the picture you create of the shot you want to make, the easier it is for the doing brain to make it happen.

Of our five senses (hearing, sight, smell, touch, and taste), sight and touch play the most significant roles in golf. The feel of the club in your hands, the feel of the slope of the terrain beneath your feet, and the information about the golf course that your eyes take in all play a major part in a successful shot. You also use balance and rhythm to help you make a coordinated, flowing golf stroke. Different emotions also affect how you move. Fear, confusion, and doubt will inhibit your golf stroke, while confidence, calmness, and positivity will encourage a fluid and effective motion.

Be careful what you wish for on the golf course. The doing brain doesn't discern any difference between good and bad pictures; it reacts to all of them. A harmful thought becomes a harmful picture that will be fulfilled with the same intensity and effort as a helpful one. You've got to accentuate the positive! If you envision the ball going over the bunker, every fiber in your being will conspire to get it over the bunker. On the other hand, should you picture the ball heading into the bunker; you better grab your pail and shovel because you're on the way to the beach.

> 'I THINK I CAN. I THINK I CAN. I THINK I CAN...'
> —The Little Engine That Could

Positive thinking leads to positive results. See where you want the ball to go. See the shot you want to make, never the one you dread. Whatever your skill level is, with pictures of optimistic outcomes you increase the chances of making your best golf stroke from that place at that time.

WHEN YOU THINK YOU CAN'T, YOU WON'T

Many golfers know they've got way too much going on in their minds but don't know how to clear out the clutter. You can quiet the noise and block out everything when you occupy your mind with what you choose to think. The less complicated the thought, like "swing to the finish," the easier it is to use. Your thinking brain will be busy with its own agenda and won't go wandering off into "How To" or "What If" land.

> "I always hit it in the water on this hole."
> > So you do.
> "I can't sink a six-footer to save my life."
> > So you don't.
> "I hate this hole. I never play it well."
> > So you won't.

What you think will directly affect how you move through your swing. Before the stroke begins, keep the thinking brain occupied with helpful ideas to block negative thoughts from creeping in and ruling the day. Use a simple thought or phrase like "breathe," or "I can do it!" to say to yourself all day. The words can differ from round to round, but it's the practice of staying with the one you start out with for the whole round that is the key to developing single-mindedness. Remember, having a thought for the day is more important than what the actual thought is.

> YOU CAN'T THINK AND HIT AT THE SAME TIME.
>
> —Yogi Berra

In his unique and inimitable way, Yogi Berra captured what scientific studies have proven to be true. When you think about what you're doing while you're doing it, you don't do whatever it is as efficiently or as well as you can when you're not thinking about it. The flow of movements that are controlled by the doing brain can easily be interrupted and altered the instant conscious thought interferes.

The consequences of talking yourself through all the steps involved during even the simplest activity all the time would be exhausting. Try this: take a step or two right now and break down every move that's involved into the most elementary segment as you walk. Has walking suddenly become labored and awkward as you think about lifting your leg, how high your knee gets raised, and how far forward you put your foot down? Can you imagine the exhaustion that instructing every move in all those actions would create every time you walk from one place to another?

The same thing happens in your golf stroke. Thinking takes time, so thinking *while* you're doing slows everything down and turns automatic moves into uncoordinated motions. Separating the golf stroke into segments and pieces to scrutinize and analyze those micro bits is counterproductive because it stops the free-flowing motion you're looking to create. It takes your focus away from the very fluidity you want your golf stroke to have.

ONLY YOU CAN KEEP THEM APART

What and when you think will have a more profound effect on the destiny of your golf ball and your scores than how far you can hit the ball or how well you putt. Thinking (instructions, reminders, warnings) should stop before movement begins. Only then can doing perform at its best: on autopilot. You've already experienced this with other physical skills you've learned, such as riding a bike, throwing a ball, typing, or playing a musical instrument. You repeat the action until you've done it so many times that your subconscious takes over. You're in glide—you don't have to think while you do whatever it is because you already know how to do it.

In every example, thinking plotted out the movements and doing repeated the action until it became automatic. Like those first few rotations of the bicycle pedals under your feet when you found your balance, what was impossible the moment before suddenly became easy and effortless. What was awkward and difficult became uncomplicated and graceful.

Do you think before you make a golf stroke? You should. Do you think throughout a golf stroke? You shouldn't! In fact, playing your best golf requires turning your thinking off during your golf stroke. The most successful golfers, the ones in the zone or at the top of the leaderboard each week, are doing just that. They've prepared themselves to have a quiet mind when they're ready to make their golf stroke. You can too when you think…*then* do.

To make a golf stroke, thinking is the preparation for doing, which is one of the many things that make the game so unique. The ball is sitting there, waiting to be hit, and you have (almost!) all the time in the world to decide when you will begin your swing. The thinking brain formulates the plan. Once you've signed off on the facts—9-iron, 115 yards left of the pin—it's all transmitted in a picture from the thinking brain to the doing brain. You react to the image in your mind of the shot you want to make, and the doing brain makes it happen.

Sounds simple enough, and it is when the thinking brain is quiet and allows the doing brain to take charge. The thinking brain always wants to add more information after you've signed off on your plan and can be bit of a smart aleck during your golf stroke. You don't have to give in to the relentless noise from your overactive brain. You can prevent the endless chatter from disrupting your golf stroke with a word, a song, or an image that fills you with a positive "I can do this" feeling.

A world-famous, Brooklyn-born cataract surgeon had his own solution for preventing the "yips." To keep his thinking brain occupied with something far from the task at hand, when he faced a (terrifying) short putt, he directed his attention away from worrying about it by singing to himself in French. There's no set rule for what to think or what to sing; you will always be the best source for finding the distraction that works for you.

The doing brain only wants that beautiful, clear picture of what to do and the chance, without interference, to react to it and excel. If you can't keep the thinking brain from interfering once your plan for the shot is set, the incessant interruptions will undermine your commitment to the shot and become the glitch behind the hitch that appears in your golf stroke.

You're in charge of putting the thinking brain on hold while the doing brain gets the job done. Keeping them apart allows the techniques you hone and the mindset you practice to come together in your stroke and your game. It all points to you. You are a thinker and a doer. You control *you*, and you are marvelous!

THE MARVELOUS YOU

"You look marvelous, darling!" and *you* are marvelous! The Marvelous You is an incomparably brilliant and remarkably complex group of natural systems within the human body that are always at work. These intricate systems automatically process information that's transmitted directly from your senses to your brain and then to your body without you having to micromanage any of it.

The Marvelous You can do an infinite number of complicated movements—like walking, typing, driving a car, or reaching for a book on the table—without constant detailed instruction. You've done these things so many times they no longer require conscious thought. These automatic actions you've learned through practice and repetition work best when you're not thinking about what you're doing while you do it. When you get out of your own way, i.e., when you're not thinking through every step of an action, you let the Marvelous You take over and lead you to your peak performance of that action.

Do you remember learning to ride a bike? You tried, you fell, you tried again, and you fell again as many times as it took you to figure it out. Your parent pushing you down the street didn't teach you how to do it. You found it, you knew it the moment you felt it, and you'll probably never forget it because you experienced what it took to learn it.

From playing the piano to playing golf, making adjustments to information gleaned from the feedback of trial and error experiences is how people learn and retain new skills. Repetition of the action allows the Marvelous You to simply do it without conscious thought.

There is a Marvelous Golfer inside everyone just waiting to be awakened. There's no end to the amazing things it can do, like hit a ball two hundred yards right down the middle of the fairway, blast out of the bunker to within a foot of the hole, or make a forty-foot putt. "You, the Marvelous Golfer," see the shot, feel the club, hear the impact, balance yourself through the motion, and know where the end of the club is just as you know where your arms and legs are without ever thinking about any of it. *You* are simply marvelous!

ATTEN-HUT!

Did you know that you physically react to suggestions and thoughts without any awareness of how and what parts of you actually move? Try this: stand up and notice how you are standing. Are you relaxed? Slouching a bit? Stomach in? Do you have more weight on one leg than the other? Are you reacting to these suggestions as you read them?

Now think of a West Point cadet. Did you instantly picture yourself standing with perfect posture? Did you straighten your spine and stand tall? Probably. Did you intend to move the way you did? Probably not, and that's the point. Did you identify which vertebrae moved as they were realigning themselves? No. Did you give yourself specific instructions about how many inches to move your neck back or raise your chin? No. Did you think about which muscle groups would lift your chest or move your shoulder blades? Probably not, and yet without any specific instructions, all these connected movements worked together instantly to improve your posture.

The picture in your mind's eye caused an immediate reaction that involved complicated muscle movements that were automatically set in motion without you thinking about what part of you to move or where to move it. You've just experienced the Marvelous You at work! Apply this idea to every golf stroke. See your stroke moving smoothly from the beginning to the ending of every drive, chip, bunker shot, and putt—and it will.

ONE PICTURE
IS WORTH A THOUSAND WORDS

Incredibly accurate shots were made from all over the golf course long before GPS systems were part of the modern-day golfer's paraphernalia. Those fabulous shots were made possible by your very own built-in range finder, just one of the many automatic systems within the Marvelous Golfing *You*. It's the brilliant system that uses your vision and instinct to compute how far away something is and tells your body how much energy to generate to get the ball to go that distance.

It works like this: you picture where the target is and the flight of the ball. If you see the ball floating over a bunker to a flagstick forty yards away and landing softly on the green, your picture tells you need a lofted club to make the shot, and the Marvelous Golfer knows which stroke can produce that shot.

Every shot begins with the picture you create in your mind of the flight of the ball or where you see it landing. One sharp image is all you need. If your vision is clouded with too many instructions and uncertainty, it's out of focus. You're not clear about the intended shot, so you make a golf stroke that matches the confusion in the picture.

When you're aware of this happening to you, back away to regroup. Bring the shot you want to make into focus with a positive picture of the ball going where you want it to go. Think it, see it, and do it. It sounds too easy, too simple, and too good to be true, but it's really what you need to do to reprogram your intentions for that shot, at that time, from that place.

PGA Tour Champion Derek Ernst, after four days of playing *Point A* golf, reflected on his winning experience in the 2013 Wells Fargo Championship, saying, "I looked where I wanted to go and I hit it there." When you "see" what you want to do, you are more likely to do it.

SEEING IS BELIEVING

Reacting solely to the pictures in their mind, blind golfers are able to make the same variety of great shots as a sighted person. Aided by their playing coaches, who verbalize the undulations on the green and the distance to the flagstick, they can see the picture in their mind of the line of a putt and sink it.

If you need more proof of the power of the Marvelous You, toss a crumpled wad of paper into a basket that's a few yards away from you. You will most likely meet with success within the first few attempts. Next, close your eyes and see the basket in your mind's eye. With your eyes closed, toss another one. This time, you're tossing the object to the picture of the basket you see in your mind. Your picture gives you all the information you need to make the toss.

If you did sink it on the first try, you were probably shocked. It's hard to believe that getting an object where you want it to go can take such little effort. And it gets even better. If you were to make the toss with a golf ball instead of the crumpled paper, the Marvelous You would adjust to the heavier weight and without conscious thought you would adjust the toss. The Marvelous You factors in the amount of energy you need to toss heavier and lighter items the same distance. You see it, and without further thought, you do it.

As you allow yourself to notice that you don't require technical information about where to put your arms or hands or when to let go of the ball for the toss, you begin to believe you can do it. You automatically make all the necessary moves without thinking your way through each step. With time and repetition, the throws become more accurate and you become more confident.

Can you imagine the freedom you'll feel when you apply this idea to your golf stroke? You have already experienced making chip shots onto the green from a variety of distances with the same club, not knowing exactly what it took to get the ball where you wanted it to go. When you're making chip shots on the range or the course, see where you want the ball to land, feel the distance, and allow your Marvelous Golfer to turn the shot you envision into a reality. You'll marvel at the ease of your stroke and the consistency of the results.

WHAT YOU SEE IS WHAT YOU GET

Has this ever happened to you? You're on the tee of the hole with a pond in front of the green that has been your nemesis for years and is the watery grave of numerous golf balls previously belonging to you. You announce to everyone that you hate this hole. Just like the last time you were here, all you can see is the water. You hear "the voice" reinforcing how negative you feel about your tee shot. "I always hit it in the water. This is the worst hole on the course." Desperate to avoid yet another ball disappearing into the drink, you deliberately and emphatically caution yourself, "Don't hit it in the water!"

Your golf stroke launches the ball—with the precision of a guided missile—directly into the water. With your shoulders slumped and your teeth clenched, you begin an immediate evaluation of what went wrong with your swing. There's no need to look for a flaw in the swing that worked on the last hole and will work just fine again very soon. The fact is the only thing you processed with your entire preparation for the shot was the water alert: exactly what you shouldn't have pictured.

You saw the water in your mind. Because the doing brain reacts to images, not words, you made a stroke that complied with your picture, and then came the inevitable "Splash!" As the ripples fanned out from the ball's entry point, in a state of frustration and despair, you mumbled, "I just knew I was going to do that!" See how smart you really are and how talented the Marvelous You really is? You knew you would hit the shot you envisioned, the one you pictured going into the water, and you did!

> WHETHER YOU THINK YOU CAN OR THINK YOU CAN'T,
> YOU'RE RIGHT.
>
> —Henry Ford

Players who already know that what you see is what you get have taught themselves to not look at the trouble. They picture where they want the ball to go, never where they don't want it to go. Just by changing your focus point, you can train the thinking brain to give the doing brain a picture of what you want to do and not what you hope to avoid. It truly is a stroke-saver to visualize the ball landing on the green, and when it does, it's so much more fun to say, "I just knew I was going to do *that*!"

If your last look down a fairway was focused on the water hazard that runs parallel to the left side of the hole, the final instruction you gave yourself about the shot was a clear picture of water on the left. You're thinking water. You're picturing water. Your thoughts are all about the water. Now it's unlikely that the ball will go anywhere but left and into the water. If this has happened to you—and honestly, what golfer hasn't had this experience—why not prepare a positive pre-shot process before you get to the ball? Look only where you want the ball to go. If you see the water, get that picture out of your mind. Back away, take a deep breath, and start your routine again.

Get back to *Point A*, where you are not looking at imagined, unwanted results. Look at the hole again and see only the enormous wide-open fairway beckoning to you. Picture the ball landing in the middle of all that greenery, and the odds will shift in favor of your ball retriever remaining in your bag and your ball arriving safely on dry land.

The constant subtle adjustments made by the Marvelous You help you achieve greater success in all your physical endeavors. Too many how-to instructions during an action get in the way of the Marvelous You, clogging up and slowing down a system that operates at its best in glide on autopilot. Keep it simple, and simply do it.

David, a *Point A* student, was practicing punch shots on the fairway 125 yards from the green. As he was doing this, he was wondering what kind of shot to use from the nearby bunker just in case the ball ever landed there. "It's the same shot" was the answer as the Pro tossed another ball into the sand. With a 9-iron in hand, David sent the ball flying to the slightly elevated green. It landed, rolled a bit, and stopped fifteen feet above the flagstick. "This is unbelievable! I never dreamed I'd be able to do that. I wonder if a pitching wedge would have made it that far?"

To answer the question and prove the point, another ball was placed in the sand and the shot was attempted. The ball flew higher and shorter, settling less than five feet below the flagstick. As they drove to the next hole, David was still amazed at the results: two great shots from the bunker to the green with two different irons. How can that be?

On the next tee, David shared a revelation with his instructor: "It must have been the Marvelous

Me at work. I didn't think about doing anything differently with my swing or my tempo when I made the second shot. I saw the shot in my mind and just did it. The Marvelous Me knew exactly how much energy it would take to make the shot with each club. All I had to do was get out of the way!"

The feedback we get from failed attempts is the information we use to improve our skills. When toddlers fall down, they are learning to stand up. When you miss several putts on the left side of the cup, you instinctively aim more to the right. Some of the best shots happen when you get out of your own way and let yourself simply do it.

IT'S ABOUT TIME

The typical round of golf (about four hours) is longer than it takes to watch the movie version (three hours and twelve minutes) of *War and Peace*. At an average flying time of three hours and twenty minutes, it's also longer than the time it took the Concorde to cross the Atlantic Ocean from New York to London.

Considering that a golf swing takes about one second from start to finish and if you include an occasional practice swing here and there in your total of swings per round, less than two minutes of your four hours on the course is spent making golf strokes. Break that down into what you do during the remaining three hours and fifty-eight minutes, and it becomes apparent that golf is a game where you, the golfer, are going to have a lot of time on your hands. Are you using your time wisely?

What do you do when you're not swinging the club? You do what every other golfer does: you walk or ride to your next shot…and you think. Compared to most other sports, golf allows an extraordinary amount of time for thinking in between actively doing the activity.

The time in between is your opportunity to stay positive and find something good in every situation. "I made solid contact even though it landed in the bunker." "This is a really slow round, but I'm so happy to be out here with my good buddies." "It may have been a grounder, but it rolled forever."

More than your mechanical skills, what you think and when you think the entire time you're on the course is the real foundation of your game. How you use the time in between your shots will become the essence, spirit, and soul of your game.

Every professional at any tournament has the technical skills to win it or he or she wouldn't be there in the first place. Beautiful swings don't guarantee tournament wins, but an effective swing coupled with a strong mind might. That's why developing your *Point A* mental game is so important and where you want to begin building your competent and confident Marvelous Golfer.

CHAPTER FOUR

IT ALL POINTS TO YOU

WHAT CAN YOU CONTROL?

Every day, many of us try to control many things that we can't. You know you can't control the car in front of you, your mother-in-law, or the slow checker in the supermarket, and yet you're reluctant to give up trying.

How about golf? What do you think you can control in your golf game? The belief that you can control your golf stroke or where your ball goes is widely held by professionals and amateurs alike. Ask any golfer these questions and the responses are usually the same:

"Can you control your golf stroke?"
"Yes, of course. That's why I practice: to be able to control my golf stroke better."

"Can you control where your ball goes?"

"Yes, some of the time. Well, I think I should have control over the ball."

"Can you control your score?"

"Yes, I control my score. I make it happen."

Sadly for many golfers, the belief that you can control where your ball goes or your golf stroke often leads to heartbreaking experiences. If the best players in the world can make mistakes and hit balls into bunkers, out of bounds, or over the green when they're playing at their best and leading a tournament, it's proof positive that even professionals can't control where the ball goes.

The results of every golf shot are a surprise that can be delightful or deflating. Many of the best golf scores happen when you least expect them, while conversely, the highest scores tend to happen when you have great expectations and want a low score so much you can almost taste it. What's really behind an unexpected low round or a gut-wrenching high one? Hopefully, you've read enough about *Point A* thinking to know the answer is that thoughts and results are an inseparable duo.

Playing golf in a *Point A* state of mind delivers lower scores and more positive experiences more often because you allow scores and birdies to simply happen rather than trying to control and force them. The truth is you can't control any of it and neither can the best golfers in the world. There are no guarantees that a stroke will be smooth, the ball will land where you want, or you'll shoot a certain score.

If you could control your stroke, it would be the same all the time, but it never is. If you could control the ball, you'd never miss a shot, yet everyone does. If you never missed a shot, you could control your score, but no one can.

Professionals demonstrate they can't get the ball to go to their target all the time. We have all seen tournament leaders miss shots that land in bunkers, out of bounds, and over the greens. Surely they didn't want to end up in these situations, nor could they have predicted they would. It's clear that even the best players in the world can only control what's within their control. Perhaps it's time to look at what is within your control in your game and put your energy into controlling what you can instead of what you can't.

YOU CAN'T CONTROL THE CHEMICALS

Did you know that your thoughts automatically trigger the release of chemicals (dopamine and serotonin) and hormones (adrenalin and cortisol) into your bloodstream that affect the way you react to situations and the way your body moves?

How these chemicals and hormones work is complex and amazing. They can cause you to freeze on the spot, unable to move a muscle. They can also give you superhuman speed and strength, temporarily providing you with the power to do things well beyond the norm. You don't even have to experience something firsthand for them to be released into your bloodstream. Simply bringing to mind the memory of a past event can cause you to shiver, get agitated, feel afraid, or experience a wave of calm. How do you feel when you imagine an intruder in your house, your favorite pet, or a putt that you must make to shoot your lowest score ever?

Tension-provoking thoughts release the chemicals and hormones that create tight muscles that quickly turn a fluid golf move into an uncoordinated motion. We're not talking rocket science here. Every thought you have affects how your body moves, so every thought you have will be reflected in your golf stroke.

There's no need to look for the answer to what went wrong by trying to fix something in your swing. It's not the stroke that broke down; it's your control of *you* that failed. Your round changed in a heartbeat because of something you thought and how you reacted to the thought. Once anxiety and fear have set in, you don't feel the same way you did a few seconds before and your body doesn't move the same way. When you hit a ball out of bounds or into the water and begin to worry that you'll never recover, the thought is enough to sabotage your next shot and perhaps several more after that.

You can't control what the chemicals and hormones do to you once you've had the thoughts that released them. However, you can choose to control you and think with *Point A* positivity to prevent your emotions from opening the floodgates that let them loose.

YOU CAN HOLD BACK THE HORMONES

Does this sound familiar? You were on the 14th hole, well into the round, and knew exactly what your score was, and it happened to be remarkably good. After a quick calculation, you realized that you had to keep playing well on the remaining holes to shoot your lowest score ever. You got so far ahead of yourself that you were already hosting the celebration. Meanwhile, back here in the present—where you had to make an actual golf stroke— you began to worry about how to do it and whether or not you could.

Distracted from the shot at hand, you were suddenly dealing with excitement and doubt and probably sending out a hormone or two in response to those emotions. The thoughts you imagine about a possible result in the future affected how you felt and how your body moved here, in the present. The golf stroke and/or putting stroke that worked so well and had already gotten you this far suddenly vanished because the good thinking that governed all those good strokes changed, and that's what changed everything.

A look into the future with expectations of controlling the score can cause unwelcomed changes even in the most well-practiced golf stroke. Scott Hoch attributes losing his chance to win the 1989 Masters, where he missed a two-foot putt for par on the 72nd hole, to thoughts of winning rather than remaining fully focused on the putt. It takes only one moment of undisciplined thought to release those chemicals and hormones and open the door that leads to distractions that allow confusion, fear, or doubt to dictate how your body moves.

One *Point A* professional reacts to thoughts that take him away from the present by laughing inwardly at them and asking, "What am I doing thinking about the final score when I'm here on the 16th hole? I don't belong there. I want to get back to this shot right here at *Point A*." The laugh, which has been shown to lead to reductions in stress hormones, releases tension and is a crucial step toward getting back to a state of calm and balance. He's soon back at *Point A,* where the focus is one stroke at a time, and his plan is to picture it, trust it, and do it.

If you should happen to stray from the present, become aware of it and remind yourself to return to *Point A* and continue to play from *Point A* to *Point A* until you hear that wonderful clinkity, kerplunkity sound of the last putt you drain on the 18th green. Believe you can control your thoughts, and with time and practice, you will.

YOU CONTROL YOU

You control everything about *you*: your attitude, preparation for the round, thoughts, emotions, self-talk, and, of the utmost importance, your reaction to each shot. There's an undeniably close relationship between how well you control *you* and how well you play. Whether you're playing for your living or a two-dollar Nassau in your favorite foursome, the following story could happen to anyone.

> A young professional was inside the cut line with a 70, 69, and 72 and was just one day away from earning his tour card. He felt positive about the day and all was going well. He was even par as he teed off at the 13th hole on the final day. He had been fearful of this hole because it just didn't fit his eye and sure enough he hooked the ball out of bounds. His temper flared and the emotions that had been tightly controlled for twelve holes unraveled into a simmering rage.
>
> He was seeing red as he teed up a provisional ball. He tried to steer the ball into the fairway but again the stroke created another hook. Luckily, this ball stayed in bounds, but he thought he now needed

a spectacular shot to make up for the miss. In his highly emotional state of mind, he made a foolish decision to try to go for the green from an awkward lie. The shot landed in the greenside bunker in a treacherous downhill lie.

Suddenly, his game began to fall apart. His mind was racing, his coordination left him and he wasn't seeing very clearly. He ended up carding a triple bogey 7 and limped in with a disappointing 76.

His golf stroke appeared to have broken down, but the real culprit that cost him his tour card was allowing fear to overcome him on that fateful 13th hole. Where his mind went triggered the sudden change in where his game went. Had he been able to gather his wits together and return to *Point A* after the first poor drive, he might have had a chance to earn his card. Instead, he left *Point A*, wandered into the future, thought about numbers instead of golf strokes, and poof! what was going great in the round suddenly went in the opposite direction.

YOU HAVE BRAINS IN YOUR HEAD.
YOU HAVE FEET IN YOUR SHOES.
YOU CAN STEER YOURSELF ANY DIRECTION YOU CHOOSE.
YOU'RE ON YOUR OWN. AND YOU KNOW WHAT YOU KNOW.
AND YOU ARE THE ONE WHO'LL DECIDE WHERE TO GO.

—Dr. Seuss, *Oh, the Places You'll Go!*

Where the ball goes is the result of your golf stroke. Your golf stroke is the result of what you were thinking before you made it. From shot to shot, every step of your journey on the course is the result of the thoughts behind the golf strokes you made along the way.

We have all read about golfers who are three down coming into the final holes suddenly able to put an end to their devastating downfall. We see golfers turn the tides and shift the momentum all the time. It doesn't happen with a swing change; it happens with a change of mind. Change your mind to change the results.

TURN ON A DIME

Were you ever going along just fine until you realized you were shooting lights out, and in that split second, your body suddenly became uncoordinated and moved as if it had been taken over by a non-golfing alien? Have you ever started out on the way to the worst round of your life when, without spending two hours on the range searching for it, the swing you "lost" on the front side appeared out of nowhere and you played flawlessly on the back nine?

From one stroke to the next, one hole to the next, the front nine to the back, or one day to the next, anyone's game can turn upside down or right side up in a heartbeat.

It can happen to anyone at any time. Is this true story similar to an experience you've had?

Penny, a competent 18-handicap player, was paired with her friend Caroline, a solid 6 with a long résumé of club championship titles. She felt intimidated by the thought of playing with a much better player but was hoping somehow to get over it and show what a good player she could be.

Caroline was anxious to get out ahead of a threesome that was about to check in with the starter. She hurried Penny from her car to the first tee, leaving not a minute for Penny to formulate a plan, swing a club, or practice a putt.

They teed off immediately, and the entire front nine went poorly for Penny. She felt unsettled, uncomfortable, and unprepared. She went from shot to shot feeling off guard and directionless, ultimately carding a discouraging 55 on the front nine. With every club she put in her hands, Penny tried to fix what she thought might be wrong with her golf stroke. She also changed what she was fixing with every shot. Each change was radical and took her farther and farther away from her natural swing movement. Making matters even worse, she felt embarrassed and disappointed to play so poorly in front of a better player.

Instead of quitting at the turn—an appealing thought that had occurred often on the front nine— Penny decided to settle down and focus on getting to *Point A*. She wanted to rid herself of the negativity that was seeping into her every thought.

She took a deep breath and with it came a clarity and calmness that didn't exist on the front nine. No more wallowing aimlessly in self-pity and despair. Her plan for the next nine holes was to first rid her mind of any thoughts of failure. She wasn't going to make up for the big numbers on the front nine. Whatever happened was over and done. She let go of her expectations to show a better golfer how well she could play.

With all that baggage jettisoned off her shoulders, she walked confidently toward the 10th tee, repeating her intention over and over again with every step she took. "Play *Point A* golf for every shot. Keep it simple." With her plan firmly in place, the turnaround in Penny's thinking immediately appeared in her stroke and her game. She enjoyed a blissfully burden-free back nine, opening with an unexpected birdie followed by two one-putt pars. With a terrific 42, she tallied a score several shots lower than normal and, unexpectedly, three strokes lower than Caroline's 45.

The ebb and flow in a round rises and falls in sync with what's going through your mind. Your thoughts can go from clear to chaotic in an instant. Caroline, the low-handicapper in this true story, didn't forget how to stay on plane or what body part to turn, nor did Penny suddenly remember. It appears that after a solid front nine, Caroline became distracted and drifted away from *Point A* thinking while Penny floundered until she found her way back to it.

The road from the first tee to the 18th green is bound to meander where you least expect it to; it's the nature of the game. You control whether or not you navigate your way around the course, making gentle turns as the day unfolds, or you allow your game and your round to turn upside down. You can manage *you*, or you can manage to fall apart. It all points to you.

LET POSITIVITY PREVAIL

Like the news crawl that runs incessantly under some newscasts, your thoughts come and go all day long. You might unintentionally allow some of them to distract you from whatever you're engaged in and some to stay in your mind longer than others. You choose which thoughts to let go by unnoticed and which thoughts to hold on to. You can opt to have a positive outlook or become the victim of your own negativity.

It's up to you to choose the thoughts that create a positive state of mind over those that will incapacitate you. Good or bad, whatever you're thinking will be reflected in how you move through your golf stroke. You control you, so it's always your choice to make: thoughts to build you up or thoughts to tear you down.

GAME WRECKERS

Negativity: "I hate this hole."

System overload: "Head down, knees bent, hips first."

Fear: "If I hit it into that bunker, I'll never get out."

Pressure: "I must make this putt or I'll be three down."

Doubt: "Did I pick the right club?"

GAME BOOSTERS

Positivity: "I can do this!"

Only one swing thought: "Swing to the finish!"

Commitment:"See it, trust it, do it."

Play from *Point A*: "One stroke at a time."

Gratitude: "I'm lucky to be here, playing golf."

Nothing stays the same. Things are either getting better or getting worse. That's why just when you proclaim, "I've got it!" ... it's gone. The bad news is that when you *are* playing well, it doesn't last forever. On the bright side, the good news is that when you're in a slump, the only way your game can go is up. No matter where you are, allow positivity to prevail and it will prevent you from over reacting to whatever the situation is.

MATTERS OF THE MIND

At a country club in one of New York's lush and beautiful suburbs, there was a long-standing tradition to award a lapel pin with a jagged line running through 100, 90, or 80 to every golfer the first time they broke the number. This is a golfer's true story about not breaking 90.

It was a friendly match. I had put together a solid front nine and was cruising along on the back, knowing I was playing well but not exactly how well. My friend had our scorecard, and I had no idea of my score. She was the reigning club champion, a seasoned golfer with years of experience and a shelf full of trophies.

As I was walking up the steps to the 17th tee, she called out, "Hey, Vicky, you're only 82 to here. If you par in, you'll break 90! You're playing great. Keep it up!"

With that carefully calculated update on where I was in my round, in the very next instant, I wasn't there anymore. I was completely out of my carefree, thought-free zone. Suddenly, I was way ahead of myself, unknowingly transported into the future.

I walked up to the next tee, playing out various dream scenarios in my mind. I saw myself telling the pro at our club, my husband, and just about anyone who would listen to my story all about my personal triumph. "Hooray! I finally broke 90."

Everything changed quicker than a chameleon changes colors. I pictured myself in the Grill Room as our club manager ceremoniously presented the pin and a glass of champagne to me. My mind went from playing my next shot to putting the prized pin on my shirt.

Poof! Visions of victory vanished with my very next stroke. Back to the present and the reality of the devastating turn the round suddenly took. I made seven on the par four 17th and five on the par three 175-yard finishing hole. A triple and a double put a swift end my dreams.

I had played the first 16 holes of the round never thinking about needing pars or birdies or trying to do anything to make them. On the 17th tee, I was suddenly playing with the stress of struggling to achieve goals that were out of my control.

I played the last two holes with my stomach in knots and my mind in complete chaos. I was totally preoccupied with fabricating different versions of how I would explain my downfall and failure. My fantasy trip into the future where I envisioned an outcome that I had no way to make happen turned

a fun and possible personal best round into a disappointing debacle.

What really happened is obvious if you look at the
thoughts that preceded the sudden change in Vicky's
game. First and foremost, someone else's game plan got
into her head and switched her focus from simply doing—
which was working just fine—to trying to par every hole.
That caused the change in her golf stroke.

Vicky left where she was, in the present, the moment
she began to envision receiving the award pin instead of
staying with the process that had worked so well for the
past sixteen holes. Although she didn't intend to change
anything technical, the results of her thinking changed
her technique. Her fears about what she must do to break
90 and the dreaded outcome if she didn't threw her completely off balance and out of kilter.

Even though she didn't earn the pin she had her
heart set on, the experience gave her an idea. She told the
club manager he should have another pin on hand to be
awarded for rounds like hers. "After all," she explained
with a huge grin on her face, "when you've come so close,
not breaking a number is as memorable as breaking it."
She answered his quizzical look with a description of
what she had in mind: "This pin should depict a bright
red heart with a jagged line drawn through the middle of it!"

TAMING A TYPE A

There's something about this game that brings out Type A behavior in almost everybody who plays it. Everyone becomes a perfectionist in pursuit of a picture-perfect and predictably consistent swing that inevitably becomes the road to endless and often exhausting fruitless hours on the range in search of something that doesn't exist.

Looking for and expecting consistency in the golf stroke or in the game itself is a fool's errand. You can bank on the fact that the only consistent thing about golf is its inconsistency. The wind, temperature, height of the grass, or speed of the greens is never exactly the same. Every shot is different, every stroke is different, every hole is different, the aggregate of the numbers you shoot in a round is different, and, every day, you are different. After four hours on the course you don't feel the same as you did when the round began.

The player with expectations of consistency plays under a veil of constant stress and experiences the impact of it as the round progresses from shot to shot and from one hole to the next. If you're playing well, you expect it to continue and the pressure to keep it up keeps on mounting.

An extremely good day affects the outcome of the next round you play. You expect it to happen again the next time you go out to play, but there are no guarantees for that scenario. If you're not playing well, your disappointment sets you up to play even worse. Expectations can put you in a lose–lose situation. This may be why it's not uncommon for a tour player who shoots 62 one day to have a difficult time repeating it with another low score the next day. Quite often, a 72 or even a 73 follows on the heels of an extraordinarily low round. The same can be said about shooting twelve shots higher than your normal score. More than likely, it was an aberration that should be forgotten immediately.

Perfect repetition and complete control of the golf stroke is impossible. Because of all the complicated movements that are part of the motion and all the variables inherent in every person's size and flexibility, every fleeting golf stroke can't be a perfect, repeatable swing. No two golf strokes or rounds are ever exactly the same.

But all you perfectionists out there can take heart. Thankfully, there is a place where you can find and practice consistency day in and day out. You can actively engage in practicing and perfecting your *Point A* thinking for as long as you are lucky enough to play the game. And most encouraging of all, there's no limit to the level of success you can achieve with it.

The distance you can hit the ball may wane with age, but the wisdom of how you think the game continues to increase and expand. Shooting your age is more a product of know-how than how far you can hit it. For most golfers, a quick exploration into what you actually can control changes how you view yourself and your surroundings on the course. You won't have to suppress the Type A golfer within once you become a *Point A* golfer, aware of how to redirect the search for perfection to a place where it can be found—in controlling *you.*

CHAPTER FIVE

POINTING YOU IN THE RIGHT DIRECTION

ALL A'S

An all-A report card can't get any better, an all-A rating can't get any higher, and golf won't be the game you love to hate when you're a *Point A* thinker. Let go of the beliefs that have been holding you back. Free up your natural golf stroke, and grow your game with these simple *Point A* tools: awareness, allowance, and acceptance.

Point A thinking directs your awareness to the present so you can be tuned in to both what's going on inside *you* and what's happening around you. It allows you to *do* instead of *trying to do* because you accept a result before it occurs. Having a *Point A* plan that's positive, simple, and within your reach is a pathway to reaping the satisfaction and delight of an all-A experience every time you play.

YOUR "A" GAME OR YOUR POINT A GAME?

Golf is a solo sport. Unlike basketball, where a teammate can grab a rebound and sink a basket, or football, where any of eleven players can recover a fumble, in golf, there's no one else around to hit a shot for you. You're never resting in the dugout waiting for your turn; you're always next at bat. You and you alone are solely responsible for every shot and every mistake. No one passed the golf ball to you. It's just sitting there, exactly where you hit it. You plan every move, and you play every shot. You're even your own referee, responsible for calling an infraction on yourself when you break a rule. You're out there on your own with no one to pass to and no one to blame.

Does this sound familiar? Things aren't going well in your round. The first few holes leave you wishing you had stayed home. You desperately look for an excuse for playing poorly. You beat yourself up every time you miss a shot, maybe even calling yourself a few self-depreciating names. You decide to write it off to not bringing your "A" game with you. You announce that it's just not your day and you really can play better. It's an easy out that you hope your playing partners will understand. But it doesn't matter whether they do or they don't because what you've really made public and, more importantly, told yourself is that you gave up on you and the rest of the round. You're excused from having to play well and have done an excellent job of reinforcing how helpless and hopeless you feel.

The round doesn't have to end that way. There's no reason to lose interest, give up, and stop caring after a few missed shots leave you doubting yourself. Instead of feeling lost and clueless, take control of managing *you* and tap into the Marvelous You to put yourself back in the driver's seat of your game. Why not leave your fictitious "A" game at home permanently and bring your *Point A* game with its *Point A* tools instead?

THE TOOLS OF THE TRADE

Point A tools are ideas to change your approach to how you think the game. How you think the game changes how you play, and it may even change *you* in the process. Awareness keeps you alert and focused. Allowing keeps you calm and prevents you from making unreasonable demands on yourself. Accepting keeps you burden-free.

AWARENESS

Everything begins with awareness. Without it, you don't know where you are or what you're thinking. When you're aware, you're in the present, more alert, and ready to give 100 percent to your shot. When you're unaware, there's a multitude of distractions that can take you away from being present without you even realizing it.

You want to be aware of your thoughts so if they happen to take you away from *Point A*, you can easily return to it. You want to be aware of the wind so you can calculate its effects on your shot. You want to be aware that you need to eat to keep your body in top form for the four hours you're on the course. You want to be aware that you can't control what your playing partner says to you, but you can control your reaction to what was said. Awareness is not a focus on these things but more of a subtle "noticing" of them. Without awareness, you can easily wind up in many unwanted places during the round. Awareness is the compass that leads you back to here and now and where you want to be.

Being aware that you are becoming upset
reminds you to take a deep breath
and get back on track.

Being aware that you see only the hazards,
redirects your focus
to the targets you want.

Being aware that you are walking too fast,
changes your pace
so you can slow down.

Awareness gives you x-ray vision into *you*. It allows you to zoom in on a clear picture of your thoughts, emotions, and how you deal with adversity of the course. While struggling through a rough patch, the highly aware golfer may right his ship within two or three strokes and sail through the rest of the round. The unaware golfer often sinks slowly into a state of despair and self-destructs hole by hole.

There are so many golfers that don't recognize until after the round is over that they needed to do something differently when they had the opportunity and that they had a *Point A* tool they could have used. They think more clearly off the course and after the round and say, "If I had just done this or that, I could've saved so many shots today."

When you see your situation on the course for what it is, it's your awareness that keeps you levelheaded. Playing with awareness lifts the fog that muddles your thinking and gives you clarity and a feeling of self-control right at the moment when you need it the most.

With awareness, you realize some playing partners' comments about your shots can have a very negative effect on your next shot. "Hey, Zach, that's your longest drive ever on this hole. I've never seen you hit it better" might sound like a compliment, but does hearing it before he's about to make his next shot really help him? Maybe yes, and maybe no. Awareness allows you to know what to listen to and what to ignore.

How do observations about you or your game affect you? An unnecessary disclosure at exactly the wrong time from a so-called friend can quickly put an end to a good score in progress, like "Joe, you've got 40 on the front and only 32 to here. All you have to do is par in and you'll break 80." Whether the observations are intended to bolster you up or tear you down, once they get into your head, comments like these can easily steer you in the wrong direction.

Awareness protects you from allowing other people's intentions to influence your thoughts. It prepares you ahead of time to notice them so you can let them go. Your determination to stick with your plan, the same one that got you to shoot 40 on the front nine, will be the coat of armor that fends off any not-so-well intentioned barbs. If you do drift away from the here and now, awareness brings you back to *Point A*.

ALLOWING

Allowing is a one-size-fits-all tool that can be applied almost anywhere in your game. It clears the way for you to *do* instead of *try*. Are you aware of how you feel when you're *trying* to swing, make a putt, par the hole, or get out of the bunker? It's a radically different feeling from simply *doing*. Allowing is the delicate bridge between trying and doing. Cross over it, and you'll go from searching for machine-like perfection in your golf stroke to letting the ball fly with the freedom and fluidity that allowing creates.

Allow

* your stroke to have a beginning and an ending.
* a deep breath to relieve tension before each shot.
* your senses to feel the weight of the club.
* yourself to forget the last shot and move on.
* yourself to have fun!

When you use this tool, without any additional energy or thought, your point of view changes. Practice allowing until it subtly becomes an automatic part of how you think. Choose allowing over trying every time, and just do it!

WINNIE THE POOH

"HAVING TROUBLE, PIGLET?"

"THE LID ON THIS JAR IS STUCK," GASPED PIGLET.

"YES, IT … IS, ISN'T IT?

"HERE, POOH, YOU OPEN IT." (POP)

"THANKS, POOH," SAID PIGLET.

"NOTHING, REALLY," SAID POOH.

"HOW DID YOU GET THAT LID OFF?" ASKED TIGGER.

"IT'S EASY," SAID POOH.

"YOU JUST TWIST ON IT LIKE THIS, UNTIL YOU CAN'T TWIST
    ANY HARDER. THEN YOU TAKE A DEEP BREATH AND, AS
    YOU LET IT OUT, TWIST. THAT'S ALL."

"LET ME TRY THAT!" YELLED TIGGER, BOUNCING INTO
    THE KITCHEN.

"WHERE'S THAT NEW JAR OF PICKLES? AH, HERE IT IS."

'TIGGER,' BEGAN PIGLET NERVOUSLY, 'I DON'T THINK
    YOU'D BETTER–'
'NOTHING TO IT,' SAID TIGGER.
'JUST TWIST, AND–'
CRASH!
'SLIPPED OUT OF MY PAW,' EXPLAINED TIGGER.
'HE TRIED TOO HARD,' SAID POOH.

—Benjamin Hoff, *The Tao of Pooh*

It's an amazing thing about trying too hard. It just doesn't work. Trying takes effort and often feels awkward. Allowing is so natural that once you've felt it, you'll wonder why you've been stuck on trying so hard for so long. Whatever your skill level, no matter what your abilities are, if you allow yourself to trust *you*, the best of you is sure to emerge.

ACCEPTING

Everything about the game of golf is unpredictable. You don't know how you'll feel the day of play, where the ball will land, how fast the greens will be, how well your opponent will play, or how the rest of the field is doing. There are no patterns in golf, so your three pars in row or your three missed putts don't predict a trend.

Accepting the uncertainties inherent in the game prepares you to deal with the unexpected, undesired, and even unimaginable shot. There's no point in getting upset about where the ball lands because there's absolutely nothing you can do about it. Nada. Zero. Zilch. Why waste your energy on something that's over and done instead of putting it into your next shot?

You'll only confuse yourself if you become emotional about where the ball lands. In an agitated state of mind, it's much more difficult to see and weigh your options and make wise choices. When you put positive energy into creating a good stroke from where you are at *Point A* instead of wishing the ball were somewhere else, you're more likely to achieve a more successful outcome.

Every shot at *Point A* is a new opportunity for success. That's exactly why every shot should be valued equally before you make it and always approached from a positive and optimistic point of view. At anytime from anywhere, you could hole out from the fairway, sink a long putt, or hit the best shot of the day. Your next shot could go anywhere, and there's no doubt it will. That's golf.

Accepting it all before any of it happens is the goal. Then, when something unwanted occurs—and it certainly will—you'll be prepared to handle it because you removed the potential stress before it had a chance to hamper your next stroke

It is what it is! Do you complain and berate yourself over a missed shot or bad luck, or do you move on to *Point A* and embrace the next challenge? The fact is, you can either critique and criticize every shot and be aggravated and miserable, or you can accept where the ball is, opt for a positive point of view, and make the best shot you can from where you are. You can only figure out what to do with the ball from where it is now, not where you think it should have been. You want to make a stroke that's free of any emotional baggage from the last shot ("Oh no! In the water again?") or any ties to a possible outcome in the future ("If I miss this putt, I have no chance of breaking 90!").

THAT LITTLE WHITE BALL WON'T MOVE
UNTIL YOU HIT IT,
AND THERE'S NOTHING YOU CAN DO
AFTER IT HAS GONE.

—Babe Didrikson Zaharias

Are you able to forget the past and play the next shot from *Point A*? It appears as though Matt Jones did in the 2014 Shell Houston Open. He won his first PGA tournament with two highly unlikely shots. The first was a forty-six-foot putt for a birdie 3 on the 18th hole to tie with Matt Kuchar and extend the tournament to a sudden-death playoff. Surely Jones didn't intend to hit his approach to the 18th hole so far from the flagstick, but he did. He accepted where it was and allowed himself to put his focus and energy into doing the best he could. He made the putt and went back to the 18th tee for the playoff. Again, his approach shot didn't seem to be what he intended. This shot missed the green, and Jones was left with a long pitch over a bunker. He accepted the situation and did the best he could from where he was, and his shot from the fairway went over the bunker and into the hole for a birdie 3 to win. Who could have predicted that?

To accept where a shot lands is not settling for mediocrity. It is your resolve to let nothing stand in the way of giving positive energy to the shot at hand. There's no room for negativity or criticism of you by you. Acceptance of wherever the ball lands and the fact that it's over and done is what sets you free and allows you to move on to *Point A*, unencumbered and ready to play your next shot.

POINT A

Playing golf from *Point A* may just be that illusive secret that really is no secret at all. *Point A* is the big enchilada, the pot of gold. It's the very heart of playing golf with you controlling your thoughts instead of your thoughts controlling you. The very idea of being at *Point A* heightens your awareness and allows you do the best you can with whatever the situation calls for.

Point A is the most powerful tool of all. The idea of *Point A* works everywhere all the time. Whether you're engaged in a conversation, reading a book, or getting ready to make a golf stroke, you must be fully there or the conversation goes nowhere, you don't remember what you read, and you can't make your best swing.

When you are emotionally detached from the results of your last shot and where your ball is going next, the quality of the shot you are making *now* will improve. Any positive pictures or trigger words will keep you at *Point A* and help you stay there. Try using the strong images of a brick wall and scissors to keep you in the present. They remind you that you can't do anything about a shot you've already made or force the ball to a target.

After you make your stroke—good or bad—see an imaginary wall behind you with the words "FORGET IT" emblazoned boldly across the bricks. If your thoughts try to take you back to the shot, you'll bump into the wall and change your mind. Use a pair of imaginary scissors and cut the imaginary emotional strings you've attached to the shot. Let your stroke have more freedom and allow the ball to just fly. When you care too much about the outcome and feel yourself steering the ball to the target, realize the ties that are binding you are your creation and yours to get rid of.

Every golf shot is completely detached from both its predecessor and its successor. Like flipping a coin, predicting what your next stroke will be based on your last one is impossible. A golf shot is born, lives, dies, and will never happen again. It doesn't matter where the ball came from, how far it traveled to get there, whether it rolled on the ground, or if it dropped down from above, it's at *Point A* when it arrives. After every shot, it is time to move on burden-free to *Point A* to prepare for the next shot.

CHAPTER SIX
POINTS OF INTEREST

POSTURE GRIP ALIGNMENT

It's common for introductory golf lessons to begin with what many professionals believe to be the fundamental ABCs of the golf stroke: the proper posture, grip, and alignment. But as you can readily see on every practice range every day, there isn't an ideal combination of all three that will fit everyone. Because golfers come in a wide variety of ages, sizes, strengths, and skills, everyone's golf stroke is different and any golf stroke can win a tournament.

There are golf champions with variations in their postures and spine angles. World famous professionals Jim Furyk, Lexi Thompson, and Bubba Watson, just to name a few, have unorthodox moves in their swings that yield winning shots time after time. There are golfers who set up to the target open, square, or closed, effortlessly making spot-on shots. The annals of the game have recorded champions who have won using all types of grips: interlocking, ten finger, overlapping, strong, neutral, weak, and more.

There are golfers with only one arm or leg who are more than able to make highly effective golf strokes. Paralyzed from the waist down after an accident in 1974, Dennis Walters proves every day that a golf stroke can be made with any posture, grip, and alignment. He puts on an astonishing display of inspirational golf shots from a swivel chair mounted to a golf cart.

All these combined variables hint at the idea that there might be something else more basic and universal in the making of a successful golf stroke than posture, grip, and alignment. *Point A* golf offers the idea that the common fundamental present in everyone's golf swing is movement, and the thoughts that generate that movement are what determines where the ball goes and how it gets there. If you want to change the results of your golf stroke, consider looking into some thoughts that will change how you move.

MOVEMENT

Without movement, there is no golf stroke. Even though the variety of body styles, skill levels, and belief systems about the golf stroke is the reason everyone moves differently through the stroke, the one thing all golfers have in common and have to do is move. The more efficiently a golfer moves through the swing, the better the results will be.

The broad concepts in *Point A* thinking that initiate the golf stroke listed below lead to a freedom and fluidity in your golf stroke that can unlock the power and beauty in your natural swing motion.

A beginning, an ending, and nothing in the middle
　　to create a fluid, whole motion.
Feel the weight of the club
　　to have an awareness of where the club is.
Swish
　　to initiate speed and freedom.
One-second stroke
　　to make the most efficient and powerful movement.
There is no ball
　　to prevent trying to hit the ball.

With one clear picture in your mind of what you want, the Marvelous You does everything possible to make it happen. For example, without any specific details, visualize the way you want the club to look through the swing, and the Marvelous You will help you bring about what you see. You can picture your favorite professional golfer and think you are him/her and allow yourself to just move.

Don't ever envision the flaws in your stroke that someone pointed out to you. If you see your stroke coming over the top, your doing brain will react to that picture and you'll do your best to make that image happen. The bottom line is that when it comes to negative thinking, you're damned if you do, so just don't!

A BEGINNING, AN ENDING, AND NOTHING IN THE MIDDLE

The golf stroke is not pieces, parts, or positions stitched together. It's not careful, deliberate, or slow. It's not executed on some imagined confining track. It's one complete movement that has a beginning, an ending, and nothing in the middle. That means you don't want to interrupt the stroke by adding anything in the middle, like hitting at the ball, holding the angle, or firing your hips. Short and long strokes, strokes in the sand, and, yes, even putting strokes all have a beginning and an ending. The ball just happens to be in the path of the stroke.

Sprinters don't end the race at the finish line. They run full speed ahead past the tape. They'd have to do something to slow down before reaching the tape if they wanted to stop at the tape, which would mean good-bye momentum and good-bye winning the race. When you envision a sprinter passing the finish line at top speed, you'll swing to the finish every time.

"Hold the finish" is a similar thought that also gets you all the way to your finish and keeps you balanced throughout the entire swing. Like the racer, the golf stroke keeps moving until the energy supply is diminished. It's loaded with power and speed and doesn't stop at the ball but keeps moving past impact all the way through to the end of the stroke. Swing to the finish was one of Rory McIlroy's first instructions from his coach, Michael Bannon, when they began working together.

FEEL THE WEIGHT OF THE CLUB

When you make a golf stroke, can you feel the weight? Not the two pounds you gained after last night's pasta dinner or the problems of the world on your shoulders—we're talking about the weight of the club.

The weight of the golf club and your awareness of swinging that weight can be a huge plus in getting the most from your golf stroke. When you feel the weight, you feel connected to the club and your balance, tempo, and timing fall into sync. You and your club become one, and you feel as if the club is a natural extension of your own body and not a foreign object.

There's an easy experiment you can try with your driver or any long club to help you feel the weight in the clubhead. With a firm grip and the clubhead pointed toward the sky, hold the club in front of you like an umbrella and carefully draw large circles in the air. Do you feel the clubhead at all? Most people don't. Loosen the grip pressure and try it again. The club should feel almost floppy as it moves in a less perfect arc. Can you feel it now? Most people do. Try firm pressure again and then light. It's really different, right? Now you get it! Experiment some more until you can feel the weight.

Now that you're aware of the weight of the club, let's take it to your stroke. Not only do clubs come in different sizes and shapes, they also have different weights. Even though the driver has the largest head and appears to be the heaviest because of that feature, it's actually the lightest. The wedges and putter are the heaviest.

Heavy or light, you want to allow the weight to swing. Don't steer, push, or muscle any club through the swing. That will cause you to tighten your grip, shorten your stroke, and prevent you from feeling anything. A stroke that begins with "I'm going to kill this one" has no feel in it—you might as well be swinging a two-by-four. The only thing that gets killed is the stroke itself and any chance of a making a best-in-my-career shot.

Let's take our mid-air example to solid ground so you can feel the amazing difference between pushing the ball with your putter and allowing the weight of the putter head to strike the ball. This convincing experiment will give you a feel with the putter that you may not have experienced before. Using your dominant hand, hold the putter at the very end of the grip and roll a few putts across the green. Putting one-handed gives you a heightened awareness of the weight of the club. You discover the weight of the putter head by allowing it to swing without any how-to instruction.

Continuing to use only one hand, grip down on the putter and sense whether you've lost the feel or if it's more intense. Did you realize that the shorter the distance between your hand and the putter head, the less feel you had with the club? That's why it's best to do this exercise holding the club at the very end while you find the feel.

Simply let the putter swing like a pendulum and feel it. With long and short putts alike, take dead aim and let the feel allow you to get the ball rolling without much calculation or effort. With every stroke, you'll become more and more aware of the weight. Change your grip pressure from firm to light and back again to firm. There's no correct grip pressure. Discovering which one is right for you is in your hands!

SWISH

A golf stroke is a physical experience. When you feel that you're moving through your swing with the grace of a ballet dancer, the stroke is effortless and smooth. The shot is solid, goes the distance, and finds your envisioned landing area. When you try to guide the club into specific positions during the golf stroke, you feel clumsy and ungainly. The swing is contrived and slow and the ball isn't often on the clubface for those shots. "I thinned it," "I fatted it," "I chunked it," and it lands anywhere but where you intended it.

Swish is a thought that frees you to move naturally and comfortably with agility and efficiency. Effortless golf strokes are powered by thinking swish. Awkward strokes are steered and confined by trying to do something in the stroke that restrains how you move.

Not sure about any of this? Erase your doubts with this simple comparison between your normal stroke and one that begins with the thought of swishing the club. Find a small patch of grass and use a driver or any long club to make a golf swing—you know, the one you make to show everyone you know where the club is supposed to be at all times. Do it a few times just to imprint how you feel during the motion. Also notice the speed of the swing as you try to keep the club on plane and get it into all the right positions.

Next, clear away the thoughts you had for your regular stroke. Think only of creating a swish sound as you make a golf stroke that has a beginning, and an ending, and nothing in the middle. Nothing else is involved here: not where the club is, not how you look, not when you should turn, and not what you should turn. You want to move quickly, making the loudest swish sound you can.

The louder the swish,
        the quicker you move.
The quicker you move,
        the quicker the club moves.
The quicker the club moves,
        the greater the clubhead speed.
The greater the clubhead speed,
        the farther the ball will go.

When your thought is to make the swish sound louder, you automatically move quicker without thinking about how to move quicker. Try swishing the clubhead over the tips of the grass. Do it again and make a louder sound. Swish a broken tee lying on the grass. Swish a clump of turf lying on the grass. Practice this easy and natural motion a few more times without a ball. Then, tee one up and allow the ball to be in the path of the next smooth swish swing you make.

        Swish has no specific path.
        Swish makes a sound.
        Swish takes one second.
        Swish has no hit in it.

There's no need to be concerned with where your shoulders, elbows, wrists, hips, or knees are during your stroke when you think *swish*. When you allow yourself to swish the club, every part of you will comfortably find where it's supposed to be during your stroke. Feel the difference? Everyone does! Even though it's a bit of a shock to discover that a golf stroke can be so simple, easy, and fun, take a moment to delight in how far and free the ball flies when it's powered by thinking swish.

ONE-SECOND STROKE

How long does it take to make a complete golf stroke from beginning to end? Three seconds, two, or maybe even one? It's hard to believe, but the answer is approximately one second. One second is all you really need to make an efficient, proficient, and graceful golf stroke. When you watch a professional tour event on TV, if you time the swings of a few players with a stopwatch you'll see that great players do it all the time.

We're talking about every kind of golf stroke: drives, chips, bunker shots, and putts. They all take about one second from start to finish. Although it seems like an impossibly short amount of time to make a full golf stroke, just having the intention to do it quickly will help rid your swing of any actions that might slow it down or inhibit its natural freedom.

The next time a well-meaning playing partner tells you to slow down, you may not want to follow that advice. When you slow down there's more time to think, which is just what you don't need. The more things you think about, the more deliberate and ineffective your slow swing will be.

You want to think *before* and *after* your golf stroke, not during it. Here's a reminder from Chapter Three that Yogi Berra said it best: "You can't think and hit at the same time." The bottom line is that one second isn't enough time to think of more than one thing, so don't!

THERE IS NO BALL

It's all too easy to get caught up in the idea of hitting the ball. After all, it's what golfers talk about. Golf magazines feature articles demonstrating how to hit the ball farther, straighter, or higher. We hear golfers say, "I'm going to the range to hit balls," "I hit the longest drive today," and "How're you hitting it?" Golf seems to be all about hitting the ball, but the relationship between the golf stroke and the ball is actually about *not* hitting it. It may sound contradictory at first, but not trying to hit the ball makes for a smoother stroke and a better shot.

If Shakespeare spent any time on the links in between writing one genius play after another, he may have pondered, "To hit or not to hit?" *Point A* offers the answer with some other thoughts to mull over that may not inspire you to write a famous play but just might help you to play famously.

Have you ever noticed that when you are not trying to hit the ball, like when you make a practice stroke before you address the ball, that stroke is fluid and feels like a sweeping motion? In your practice stroke without the ball, you weren't hitting anything. You were simply making a golf stroke from beginning to end, so you didn't try to stop it anywhere. If *there is no ball*, there is nothing to hit. If there's nothing to hit, you make an uninterrupted stroke that propels the ball forward because it just happens to be in the path of the moving clubhead. To feel that same freedom with every type of shot—drives, chips, and putts—make all your golf strokes with your (no ball) practice stroke.

SAVE YOUR LIST FOR THE LAUNDRY

Is part of your pre-shot preparation to check off items on a lengthy list of all the things you feel you must remember while you're making your stroke? Do you recite them nervously before every shot, hoping you won't forget anything? Lists are good for Christmas gifts and supermarket shopping, but they're not very good for your golf. Does your personal pre-shot to-do inventory resemble this one?

* Keep your head down.
* Take it back inside.
* Cock your wrists.
* Bend your knees.

* Lead with your hips.
* Keep your right elbow tucked.
* Stay on plane.

Are you smiling because some of these are on your list too, and maybe you even have a few more? The longer the list, the less you remember and the more you worry about forgetting something important. A lengthy and demanding message sent from the thinking brain to the doing brain becomes an erratic and befuddled golf stroke. Keep it simple!

Can you really control and execute multiple commands at once in just one second? Most likely, you can't. How many things can you think of in one second? How many things can you do in one second? Not many, and that's the point. You've heard it before, everyone has: you can only do one thing at a time. Why fight the truth and complicate your golf stroke with more than one thought? Thinking about your stroke or adding multiple commands to it while the stroke is in motion makes it overly deliberate and artificial, which is exactly what you don't want it to be.

ONE A DAY

Point A golf strokes are set in motion by a picture that allows you to make a smooth swing with no conscious thought to "move this" or "turn that." A pre-shot thought like swish causes you to make a stroke that "moves this" and "turns that" without you having to think about it. Instead of a list of distracting and detailed instructions, make one power-packed *Point A* broad concept the engine behind golf strokes that create greater clubhead speed and a natural follow-through to the finish.

Swish.
There is no ball.
One second stroke.
Feel the weight of the club.
A beginning and an ending and nothing in the middle.

The thought you choose for a round isn't as important as the fact that you have a thought and you intend to stick with it. Wherever your golf stroke is now, you'll guide it to the next level and make it more efficient, effective, and effortless with any of these stroke-liberating thoughts. Take one a day to the range or the course and they'll be the vitamins that energize your swing and revitalize your game.

CHAPTER SEVEN

MAKING THE POINT

CHANGE YOUR SWING
OR
CHANGE YOUR MIND

You've seen it, we all have: a top professional is making a swing change. It's diagrammed in slow motion on TV like a winning football play while the commentator shows the viewers how the club is coming from a steeper path or how the knee or some other body part is working differently. What you don't see is the professional practicing that swing modification for hours, weeks, and even months. Some little changes can take years to incorporate into a swing, yet the information is shared so casually with the TV audience that you accept the idea that this apparently simple and necessary adjustment will improve the professional's game. You assume if it's good for the pro, it must be good for you. Why would the famous commentator, a professional golfer as well, take so much time to show exactly what needed changing if it weren't going to help other golfers learn how to make a better swing?

You mull over whether or not this precious little nugget of information will be beneficial to you, and within seconds, you decide to give it a try. You think this might just be exactly what you need. You're ready to abandon your old swing and work on a new grip, posture, or takeaway. You practice it successfully for a while and believe after persevering for an hour or so that you've got it. The balls are flying off the clubface. Your swing feels like you're cutting butter, and you're thrilled. You're sure this is going to be the greatest thing that's ever happened to your game.

You leave the practice tee believing in your newly reconstructed and improved swing but when you take it to the course, you find that you've been shockingly thrust into a no man's land where your old swing isn't what it was and your new swing is nowhere in sight.

Instead of advancing your game one step forward, you've taken it two steps back. You discover that learning a fractional part of a golf motion that looked so easy on TV might not become an integral part of your stroke and your game until you've practice it for a very long time, which is not at all what you expected. Also possible is the fact that this move, whatever it is, may not be a move that can possibly help your swing, no matter how much time you put into working on it.

Like almost every other golfer, you probably have a love–hate relationship with the game. You love how you feel after a good round, and you hate yourself after a bad one. You'll play as often as you can anywhere you can in almost any kind of weather. You're always on the lookout for the latest technologically advanced club, training aid, or swing change that guarantees to lower your handicap to a number you can only dream about. With every tip you try or gadget you buy, you ride waves of fulfillment and frustration that leave you coming back for more as the new fix fizzles out.

You watch golf videos that demonstrate how to hit it far, chip it close, blast it out, and putt it in. You keep trying to fix something ascribed by a topnotch instructor to be technically wrong with your swing. When you're off your game, you're just fragile and desperate enough to try anything. You can't stay away, even in your worst slump, because you really do love playing golf and honestly believe there's something somewhere that will somehow help you conquer whatever it is that keeps you from getting better. And there is. And it's simple. Simply change your mind.

FUNDAMENTALLY SPEAKING

A lasting swing change begins in your head, not in your hands or hips. If you want to change your technique, begin with looking at your beliefs about the golf stroke. As you stand over the ball, are the instructions you give yourself holding you back or advancing your skills? What you *believe* you are supposed to do with the golf club and how your body is supposed to move will either produce a fluid, effective stroke or an uncoordinated attempt to hit the ball from one spot to the next.

In the following story, which golfer are you?

Lauren and Ken believe that to improve their game, they constantly need to fix their golf stroke. Lauren's swing is slow and measured and looks as if she is steering it where it's supposed to go. She was told that to stop coming over the top, she needed to work on her fundamentals like holding her hands a certain way or moving her shoulder at a specific time in a specific direction during the downswing. Ken is so focused on carefully moving the club along an imaginary path that he hardly uses the powerful muscles in his core during the stroke. He is so certain that he can't swing a golf club properly without first mastering keeping the club on plane, it's all he works at when he practices.

They were side by side on the range one day, practicing next to their friend, Jackson. Soon, everyone was chatting and weighing in on common swing flaws and fundamentals. Jackson is a *Point A* golfer. When Lauren and Ken asked him what his fundamentals were, he paused a moment and replied that he had only one. Shocked by Jackson's inconceivable response,

Ken couldn't help but question it. "Only one? That's too easy and way too simple. Our list focuses on what parts of the body are supposed to be still or moving and also getting them to be in right place at the right time of the swing."

Jackson said thinking swish was all he needed in order to make stroke after solid stroke and get to the finish without having to think about anything else. Jackson's "one thought" fundamental was as far away from working on a list of fundamentals as it could be, so Ken and Lauren were very skeptical and hesitant to even consider the idea. But, as you probably already know, golfers belong to a special family of fanatics that will try anything in hopes that it might help. So, when they returned to their spots on the range, they surreptitiously began making golf strokes thinking swish.

Lauren's beautiful and flowing swing was so startling to her she couldn't contain her delight. The "wow" she exclaimed turned a few heads in her direction. "That was so much quicker than I have ever been able to swing a club. I actually finished the swing facing the 125-yard marker and I didn't lose my balance. I never thought I could do any of that without thinking of everything I'm supposed to remember. I can't believe a golf stroke could feel so effortless. Where has this awesome swing been hiding?"

Ken's swing made such a loud swishing noise that it startled him. "I've never felt the club move so quickly. One concept and one word—this can't be right. It's way too easy. There is so much less to think about it feels as though there is nothing to think about. My back doesn't hurt. It feels so comfortable to swing a club this way and a huge relief not to have to try to keep the club on plane."

Lauren summed up the whole experience in one sentence. "You know, I think this is fundamentally fabulous!" Jackson turned and smiled at them. They smiled back and continued to practice, this time experimenting with high and low shots, long and short shots, and having the best time they'd ever had on the driving range.

THINK BIG

Look at your stroke through a wide-angle lens and see how thinking a broad concept promotes liberating and reliable changes in your natural golf stroke to simply happen. Because your golf stroke begins with a picture, it's so important to see the swing you want, not the one you don't. The big picture concepts in *Point A* thinking don't restrict natural movement; they actually encourage it.

When your picture is of a beautiful swing moving from beginning to end, the Marvelous You will create the fluid swing that matches your picture. Without the interference and encumbrances of detailed how-to instructions, big picture ideas allow your golf stroke to move gracefully from start to finish.

For example, to create clubhead speed, if your thought is swish instead of *hit it harder*, without trying to move any quicker, you will. If you don't focus on exactly what you want to change but have one broad *Point A* concept in mind instead, you allow a move rather than force it. There's no added effort that way, and you seamlessly make changes that enhance your own natural golf stroke and improve everything about it: efficiency, rhythm, and tempo.

For many golfers, concentrating on an isolated specific move in their golf stroke is distracting and slows the stroke down. Because thinking takes time, they lose the flow of the motion when they concentrate on one little part of the whole. Even worse, the desire to make an exact move at an exact moment in a golf stroke can add unwanted and uncontrollable jerky moves to it.

> YOU CAN'T DIVIDE A SWING INTO PARTS
> AND STILL HAVE A SWING.
> A CAT IS A CAT.
> IF YOU DISSECT IT
> YOU'LL HAVE ALL THE BLOODY PARTS,
> BUT YOU WON'T HAVE A CAT.
>
> —Ernest Jones

No matter what you start out with, once it's in pieces, you can't make it whole again. All the king's horses couldn't put Humpty back together again, and all the king's men can't make eight slices of pizza become a whole pie after it's been cut. Most golfers have a difficult time trying to stitch their swings back into their natural fluid motion once they've taken them apart, and with good reason.

Think whole ideas to have a whole one-piece swing. It sounds simple and it is, and you're going to love the results. Every broad idea in *Point A* creates a big picture that is the impetus for a comfortable and quick motion through the golf stroke. Change your mindset to change your swing.

ONE OF A KIND

Making a golf stroke uses thirteen major joints and most of the muscles in your body. There are just too many moving parts and emotional variables involved in the complex motion of a golf swing to expect to make one stroke the exact replica of any other. But you still want to believe that there can be something consistent and repeatable about your stroke, right? Take heart, dear golfer, because there is. You can't control and replicate exact golf strokes, but you can control the thoughts that allow and encourage the kind of fluid golf strokes that can deliver the shots you desire more often.

After a good stroke, you (and every other golfer) want to bottle it and save the know-how forever. You think, "What did I do on that shot to make it so good?" and try to duplicate it on the next swing. To make it just a tad better, you add more thoughts and must dos that weren't in the swing you're planning to copy. It may be human nature to want to continually tweak something and constantly improve it, but in a golf stroke that's supposed to be a copy of the one before it, it's not a very good idea.

If a professional were to tee up ten balls in a row, he'd have no idea how many or which ones he'd hit well nor whether the stroke would be smooth or uncoordinated. What he would be certain of is that each stroke would be slightly different. No single shot is exactly like any other. If they could all be identical in every way, wouldn't everyone be able to sink a thirty-foot putt or make the same hole-in-one time after time after time? Basketball shots from the foul line and tennis serves fall into the same no-carbon-copy-possible category. Just like every time you sign your name, each golf stroke is slightly different enough to make it unique.

Even though it seems to be an unlikely comparison, let's look at signing your name and making a golf stroke. Even though the physical actions required to sign your name involve simply moving your hand and arm, it's still quite difficult to repeat the exact same signature time after time.

It requires very little concentration to write your signature on a piece of paper. Do it now and notice how effortlessly your hand moves and how you don't have to think about which letters go where. Try to trace it a few times, careful to keep the pen exactly on the lines of the original. Were you able do it? Most people can't. Even if you could, it would be a slow, deliberate, and laborious effort that wouldn't yield the same result each time you did it.

Learning to think "I have this one shot, I'm going to do it to the best of my ability and then, when it is over, I'm going to move on and do it again" is the practice of seeing each shot as separate from any another. It is an extremely important discipline to master because each stroke has nothing to do with the last stroke or the next stroke. A golf stroke is its own unique movement, so trying to connect shots only brings frustration.

You want to train yourself to *not* have any expectations. After you make a good shot, the tendency is to immediately try to replicate it. When you do that, you create an expectation for that stroke and you try to do it "just so," and in doing so, you simply mess up the motion. Instead, set the club behind the ball and move (make your stroke). Then, again with no expectations, on the next shot, set the club behind the ball and move. Once again, you have no expectations. Repeat the steps with every shot: "hit it and move on" without judging or evaluating the results. This type of training develops your belief that you can do it because you have done it before.

The process of moving from one shot to the next is the essence of playing one shot at a time, from *Point A* to *Point A*. Without expectations, your belief is that even though you do not know what is going to happen on any shot, the chances are that the results will be all right. Remember the old adage: to gain control you must lose control. In giving up control in this manner, you will have the most pleasant surprises.

MISS OR MISTAKE?

Everyone hits shots that are not perfect, so it is certain there will be some unwanted outcomes in every round. Have you ever seen a tournament leader hit it in the water, over the green, or into a greenside bunker during the finishing holes? It happens all the time. What's your typical reaction to an errant shot in your round? Do you accept it as a missed shot and move on or do you immediately critique it, analyze what went wrong and then obsess over trying to fix it before your next turn to play?

Missed shots are random events; forget them and move on. Mistakes occur over and over again and require your attention—the sooner, the better. When you are aware that there is difference between a miss and a mistake, you can be more levelheaded with your approach to your next shot, which is usually very different from the one you just missed—and is now the only shot that matters. When you see the same miss often enough, it's a mistake and time to make an adjustment or book a lesson with the nearest PGA professional and get help. There's no point in grooving an ineffective move in your stroke by repeating the same mistake over and over again. Classify a poor shot as either a miss or a mistake, and you'll find you are less inclined to be angry about it because you have a plan for how to deal with either situation.

A missed shot could be a hook, a slice, a shank, or a chunk, and usually there's a different reason for each of the different shots you missed. One time the club was too far inside on the way back or the clubface was too closed. Another time you were distracted by a noise or a thought or you simply picked the wrong club for the job. The question is—what are you going to do about it?

Every poor shot in golf should be considered a miss, something to *not* react to. You just step up to the next one, set up as usual, and continue to play. When there are at least three of the "same" misses, you can begin to see it as a mistake and realize you need to make a change. This allows you to work on a specific broad idea for your motion without trying to "fix" something with a new and different change every time you swing the club.

When you stub your toe, do you stop and analyze why it happened? Do you try to fix the cause, or do you just say ouch and move on? The message is pretty clear: Treat your missed golf shot like your stubbed toe. Think of it as an accident. Don't delve into what happened or get distracted by becoming preoccupied with trying to fix it. Assume it won't happen again and forget about it! It would be a very different story if you were to continually stub your toe on the same chair. After a while, wouldn't you decide to adjust where the chair is and move it out of your path? Be just as sensible with your golf stroke. Identify your mistakes, and move them out of your stroke and your game.

A miss is a miss is a miss. Accept it when it happens, and yield to the capricious nature of the game so you can be more forgiving and kinder to yourself. You can choose not to panic about what should have been or what could have been. You can't make up for lost shots, but you can make the choice to be 100 percent committed to your next shot at *Point A* and give it your best effort.

THE TIP OF YOUR NOSE

Professionals and low-handicappers will tell you that when they're playing their best, they are thinking of nothing. What most amateurs don't understand is that the road to thinking of nothing is as far from nothing as you can get. It's paved with hours of practicing how *not* to think consciously while you are making a golf stroke. It's hard to grasp this idea, but everything a golfer learns should lead toward being able to think of nothing during the stroke.

The conundrum is that you're always thinking of something. So if you're always thinking of something, how can you think of nothing? This is not a trick question and the answer is straightforward and clear. To think of nothing actually means not to think of anything that can interfere with your natural stroke and rhythm. If you've taken tons of lessons, read every how-to golf article you can get your hands on, or seen hours of videos, you still may not have come across the idea that thinking of something non-golf or swing related during your golf stroke could help you make a more effective and freer stroke.

It's hard for most golfers to accept that it's actually easier to make a smoother stroke without the swing-inhibiting thoughts that keep it from being a flowing motion. If you want proof, follow PGA professional Jack Conrad's instruction to think of the tip of your nose while you make your stroke. What does the tip of your nose have to do with executing a golf swing? Absolutely nothing, and that's the point! Make just one swing while you're thinking of something not related to making your golf stroke and you will be amazed at how different it feels. With the very first flowing and maybe even quicker stroke you make, you immediately realize that what you need to think might be changed forever. It's a perfect example of how thinking about nothing by thinking about something that has nothing to do with making your golf stroke can set you free.

Are you asking how you can possibly make an easy, beautiful, and effective golf stroke without all your normal, important how-to reminders? It works because a non-specific thought about where your wrists, elbows, knees, etc., are during the swing quiets your mind. It keeps "Left arm straight," "Don't mess up again," or "What if I miss?" from distracting you while you're making your stroke. The tip of your nose is only the tip of an iceberg that runs deep with possibilities.

CHAPTER EIGHT

THE TURNING POINT

HOME ON THE RANGE
BUT NOT ON THE COURSE?

So many golfers ask, "Why is it so difficult to take my game from the range to the course? Why is everything so easy there and so difficult on the course?" The answer is simple: You aren't the same *you* in both places. Your thoughts and emotions reflect how you feel about where you are, and the range and the course are dramatically different environments. But you can be the same you in both places or, at least, minimize some of the differences.

What many golfers have never taken into account is how each environment affects how they feel and how that directly influences the stroke that is made. Did you know that what you think before a shot could change the degree of tension in your muscles as you move through your stroke? Your thoughts create chemicals that are released into your blood stream that can change how you feel and alter how your body will react in your golf stroke. It has been documented that stress hormones, such as cortisol and adrenaline, can change your coordination and tend to make you move quicker than you normally do.

How do you feel before you make your stroke on the range? Is the stroke full of nervous jitters or a calmness that allows your body to perform at its best? How do you react to a missed shot on the range? Do you react the same way when you miss a shot on the course? You may be surprised by your answers as you become aware of *you* on the range vs. *you* on the course. It's time to notice how your feelings in both environments feed your failures and successes.

You can learn how to be ready to deal with situations on the course before they occur. It takes a plan and practice to be prepared to *not* react any differently, no matter where you are. With *Point A* thinking, you can react to shots and situations on the course with the same evenness you feel on the range.

SAFE AND SECURE OR SCARED SILLY?

On the range, you're almost invisible. No one is very interested in what you're practicing or how well you're doing. Many golfers feel threatened and exposed when they're away from the safety and shelter they feel on the range. In contrast, on the course, people are looking at you. Some of them (family, friends, and fans) are expecting you to play well. As a matter of fact, you may think everyone out there is watching you. Suddenly, you're in the middle of a spotlight on you and your golf stroke.

As you head from the security of the range toward the first tee, you become vulnerable to demons you never knew you had or have never given a second thought to before. You feel self-conscious and exposed—as if you were taking a shower in the middle of Grand Central Station and some prankster pulled the curtain aside.

In contrast, the practice range is an all-forgiving safety zone devoid of any punishment or embarrassment. Missed shots don't matter, and strokes don't count. You are hitting from the same spot all the time to a target that has no obstacles around it to intimidate you. There's no water, trees, or bunkers to add doubt to your stroke. You feel unthreatened, uninhibited, and unflappable.

You're in a private paradise of multiple mulligans! You swing away to your heart's content with no concern about the outcome of any shot. There are no consequences, so if you don't like a shot, you tee up another one. In this safe and reliable setting, it's easy to feel secure and fly flawless 7-iron shots to a ball-covered landing area over and over again.

Missing a shot or two on the range means nothing, but on the course, the same misses can mean everything to you. Those misses gradually shave away the sense of security you felt on the range. You feel compelled to fix your stroke with a new idea. It might work for a hole or two, but then, you miss again, so you fix it again and yet again. Each additional Band-Aid takes you further and further away from trusting yourself, and suddenly, you've successfully blown a gaping hole in your confidence.

On the course, you can count on everything changing all the time. The golf course never plays the same, and conditions even vary from the front nine to the back. Pin placements, the wind, the weather, and the speed of the greens add constant variability to your game. You're out in the open with no place to hide. There are other golfers with you who see and often care about every shot you make. Everything that happens on the course is unpredictable, and potential dangers are lurking everywhere. You are always teetering on the brink of a possible botched shot that could lead to a severe case of fear of failure. You can't replay a shot or practice it until you're satisfied with it, and there are no mulligans in the real game. It's frightening to contemplate the finality of each and every shot.

While what feels like the whole world is watching, even people who are superstars brimming with confidence when they are the center of attention off the course have difficulty coping with their fears and anxieties when it's their turn to play. It's a part of golf that's more than enough to fray the nerves of a normally calm person. For some golfers, it's the reason they love the game, while for others, it's the very reason they don't.

SINK OR SWIM?

Michael Phelps, one of the greatest Olympians of all time and winner of twenty-two medals, decided to take up golf after his retirement from professional swimming. Many seasoned golfers had great empathy for him when he shared his feelings of abject fear to be playing in a pro-am before the 2012 Ryder Cup at Medinah Country Club. A few minutes before he would tee it up with several PGA professionals, he said, "I was scared out of my mind. I could feel it kind of in my stomach." Phelps remarked that never in his thirteen years on the international swimming stage did he feel as nervous as he did before that pro-am scramble. In an interview with Karen Crouse (*New York Times*, September 25, 2012), he said his worst case of competition jitters occurred at his first event in the 2004 Athens Games before swimming the 400-meter individual medley. Phelps shared that he was "a thousand times more nervous" before playing in the Medinah pro-am.

What is it about this game that reduces even a celebrated world-class athlete to a state of fear and doubt before striking a ball that isn't even moving? The answer lies in what goes on in a golfer's mind well before the golf stroke begins.

If you're like Michael and so many other golfers, you want to know what you can do to overcome your jitters and get those butterflies in your stomach to calm down or, at least, fly in formation. How do you get past your need to prove yourself on each shot? How can you enjoy every step of learning to play without the debilitating results of self-imposed embarrassment? Once again, it is all about you, and you are 100 percent in charge of whether you sink or swim. Even if you are a world-class tennis player, surgeon, lawyer, mechanic, or swimmer, don't expect that you can instantly become a world-class golfer. Accept that just like whatever it is you're already accomplished in, learning golf is a process that takes time and experience. Allow yourself to enjoy the journey and have some fun as you grow yourself and your game.

The course can be perceived as a battlefield where every stroke counts, there's a score at risk, and a target to miss, or a safe haven where you can develop *Point A* thinking, explore creative shot-making, and experience the pure joy of making the shot you envisioned. It's all in your point of view. *Point A* allows you to be the same *you* on the range and on the course. Every time you play, the golf course offers you the opportunity to practice *Point A* thinking, where you can put the time you spent on the range into your game.

PLAN AHEAD

Benjamin Franklin had a bigger picture than golf in mind when he coined the connection, "If you fail to plan, you are planning to fail." No doubt you've already had an experience or two that convinced you that this famous observation applies to almost everything everywhere in life. Having a plan in place and knowing what you'll say to yourself after a missed shot before it happens is the best prevention for a destructive free fall from trusting yourself.

Your plan keeps you calm so you can carry on no matter what happens. Instead of calling yourself a stupid idiot and getting irritated about where the ball is (or isn't), you'll keep your blood pressure down and your spirits up when mistakes happen. *Point A* gives you a three-point strategy for how to think, what to think, and when to think throughout your round. In golf, planning ahead is the foundation that solid rounds are built upon.

1. Have a plan for thoughts before a shot:
   picture it, and commit to it.

2. Have a plan for thoughts after a shot:
   notice it, accept it, and move on.

3. Have a plan for the time in between:
   stay positively distracted.

Before

      Your plan before each shot is always the same. Take in the information, create a picture of the shot, make a decision about how you want to make it, feel good about it, and commit to it. Allow yourself to make the best stroke you can from this place at this time, trusting that wherever the ball goes, you'll be able to handle it.

After

Your plan after each shot is to be detached from the outcome. Watch the ball with as little emotion as possible and move on to *Point A*. Plan how you'll react to all your shots before you get to the golf course so you can keep your emotions from running away with you when you make or miss a shot. No one intends to miss a shot, but it happens to everyone. Missed shots are a part of the game, so be prepared to react in a way that doesn't hurt you when it happens. The *Point A* plan for reacting to errant shots before they take place takes you right back to *Point A* and on track to make good shots after you miss one. Then, you won't be overly elated or deflated, staying steady and even-tempered throughout the round.

In between

Some competitive players use the time to focus on mindful breathing. They might just notice their breath going in and out as they walk. Club golfers might use the time to talk about the news, their social plans, or what their children and grandchildren are up to. Some golfers like to hum a favorite tune, and some find it the ideal time to tell jokes.

Others use the time in between to appreciate their good fortune to be in such a beautiful place with the added bonus of playing the great game of golf there. People who regularly practice gratitude by taking time to notice the things they're thankful for feel happier, sleep better, and are generally less stressed than their ungrateful compatriots. Simply taking a few seconds to think of three things you're grateful for is an easy and effective prevention to carding an unwanted number.

The time in between shots is one of the many things that makes golf so special and unique. There's no other game where you can share hours of time with buddies, a teammate, or even an opponent while the game is in progress. It might also just be the only game where a food cart delivers a wide variety of snacks and beverages to the players, not the spectators, during the game.

Any plan will surpass no plan. Negative thoughts can't creep into your mind when your strategy is to have what you will think and when you will think solidly in place before the round begins. Organize your thoughts the night before, during your drive to the course, or on the range as you warm up. As long as you actually have a plan in place before you get to the first tee, you're more than good to go. Your plan for every shot can be as simple as thinking swish, the ball is always at *Point A*, the stroke has a beginning, an ending, and nothing in the middle, or anything else you choose for that day.

THE PLAN IS YOUR INTENTION

Making a New Year's resolution with no intention to follow through on it is nothing more than wishful thinking and a dream that can't come true. You may declare you want to lose weight, but you won't lose an inch by cutting carbs if you can't say no to dessert. You know you won't be able to shed an ounce if your plan is to add daily exercise to your routine and you don't actually do it. There's little sense in planning to go to the gym if the gym is too hard to get to or you simply don't like working out.

It's the same "no result" in golf when your plan includes things you're not assured of accomplishing. Your plan is the blueprint for how you intend to achieve your desired objective so make it easy to repeat and hard to forget. You'll feel positive and good about any plan within your capabilities because you'll constantly be experiencing the positive feedback of success. Keep it simple and it will keep you engrossed in what you're doing and interested in staying in your process.

THE PLAN BECOMES YOUR PROCESS

Managing yourself on the golf course begins with a plan. The purpose of the plan is to occupy yourself with something that prevents your mind from wandering off into Doubtville, Anxietyland, or the nearest fix-it shop. Choose a short-term goal that is realistic, reachable, and repeatable, like "hold my finish" on every shot. Avoid a plan that's totally unpredictable, like hitting fairways and greens or what score you want to shoot.

Here's how it works: before the round begins, along with your *Point A* tools, pick a simple task, (like visualizing every shot, holding your finish, or taking a breath before each stroke) to use throughout the day. Be sure the task is something you want to get better at that's easy enough to do and just hard enough to be challenging. Commit to doing it every shot.

If you watch Jason Day and many other professionals playing a tournament round, you'll notice they take a deep breath before every shot. It's a habit for them now, but taking deep, tension-releasing breaths starts out as a simple task for everyone.

Deep breathing is more than relaxing. It has been scientifically proven to have a beneficial effect on the heart, brain, digestive tract, and immune system. You won't have to remind yourself to do it as often over time, and through repetition, the action requires no effort at all.

YOUR PROCESS IS THE
EXECUTION OF THE PLAN

Your process is the actions that carry out your plan. If your goal is to lose weight, eating less sugar, actually taking a walk every day, or getting to the gym three times a week without fail is your process to achieve it. The key to making it all work in your golf game, like for everything else in your life, is to have a plan that is within your reach and the determination to stay the course and do it.

Rory McIlroy revealed his plan for the 2014 British Open at his highly anticipated post-win press conference. Everyone wanted to know what he was thinking on his four-day journey to becoming the 6th player, going wire-to-wire leading the tournament, to win it. He said his plan was to think of two simple trigger words throughout the tournament: *process* and *spot*. The process was to "focus on 'don't care about the result, just really get into the process'" (Kay, 2014). The plan for every putt was to pick a spot on the green and roll the ball over it. He said he knew the end result would be okay if he stayed within his process and in the present. He wasn't thinking about results or what other players were doing. It was his focus on the two simple words, *process* and *spot*, that kept him in the present and in the moment.

Point A thinking helps you use your process to fulfill your plan because when you're at *Point A*, you are in the present, making good decisions and the best swing you can make at that time from that place.

GIVE EVERYTHING THE SAME EVERYTHING

It doesn't matter if it's your best drive ever or the putt that ran out of gas on the edge of the cup, every shot adds one stroke to your score. No matter how beautiful or bad, how long or short, or how high or low any shot is, each one becomes a number in your score. Because each shot becomes equal to every other shot on your scorecard, every shot deserves the same everything before you make it. Be an equal opportunity golfer. Give each shot the same opportunity to be treated with equal importance before you make it. Give every shot the same:

Process:
> Give each shot the same routine.

Intention:
> Give each stroke the same commitment.

Intensity:
> Give each stroke the same energy.

Thought:
> Give each stroke the same consistency.

No Thought:
> Give each stroke the same quiet space.

Freedom:

Give each stroke the same "let it go" feeling.

Ending:

Give each stroke the same balanced finish.

Reaction:

Give each shot the same acceptance.

As tempting as it is to want to incorporate all these ideas into your next round and get better faster, trust and respect the basic tenet of *Point A* golf and remember to keep it simple. Embrace these concepts one at a time. With time and repetition, you'll effortlessly be honing an essential skill every time you play and each one will become an integral and automatic part of your game. Then, you'll be able to give them no thought at all!

LESS IS MORE

Robert was a *Point A* student. He heard "a beginning, an ending, and nothing in the middle" more times than he could count but recently admitted to never paying much attention to it. He said he never bothered to use it in his game. But after attending a seminar on *Point A* thinking he decided it was time to see if using that idea would change anything for him. The next day he made it part of his game plan, and to his complete surprise and utter delight, it worked immediately. His golf stroke became more fluid and he easily got to the finish every time.

So, Robert did what many golfers do. He decided he could add a little something more to make the results even better. Not surprisingly, that's when everything fell apart. The physical freedom of making effortless golf strokes was gone. In an instant, his game reverted back to the way he played before his only plan was to simply have one idea for the round. It's plain to see the simple "only one thought" plan had faded and his brain was swirling with so many thoughts that none of them worked. Although this is a short story, hopefully its powerful message will stay with you a very long time.

COMPARTMENTALIZE YOUR CARD

Some golfers absorb the idea of using tasks more easily when there is a tangible way to apply them. One way to put your plan into action is to draw a line after every three holes on your scorecard and use only one task to play each three-hole segment. Dividing eighteen holes into smaller segments allows you to compartmentalize your plan and work on something for a shorter amount of time.

You can change your thoughts and regroup after three holes if the task isn't working for you, or if it is, use it again to play the next three. You'll still be gaining expertise in the discipline of training your mind to stay on only one thought. Playing the whole round with one thought is not as overwhelming when you get to reboot and commit to a new task every three holes.

When you've reached a comfort level with the three-hole exercise, draw a line after every six holes and repeat the process. Playing golf for four hours is infinitely more satisfying, rewarding, and much more fun when you choose a task for the round and build your game plan on its simplicity. Eventually, you will be able to stay with your game plan for the whole day. You'll stay engaged in your round whether it's one of your better days or one of those less desirable yet inevitable experiences we all have had and need to forget!

PRACTICE IS PLAYING
PLAYING IS PRACTICE

Everyone also knows that when you love what you're doing, you never want to stop. Don't work on your game at the range, love practicing it there with passion and a plan. Keep in mind that practice is not a search for perfection. Perfect is temporary and fleeting. Practice is a journey that is a source of rewards, both anticipated and surprising.

The range and the course are a circle. The golf course is where you'll discover the shots you want to work on at the range, and the range is where you'll practice those shots for the course. At your next practice, there's no reason to concentrate on your wood and hybrid shots if your look-back after your round was "I had way too many putts." Don't bother going to the putting green if you "couldn't get out of a bunker with a snow shovel today." "Not one drive in the fairway!" is probably not a ticket to the chipping green. Let your last round be your guide to what you practice. Notice where your game came up short, and invest your time on that aspect of it.

THE MORE I PRACTICE, THE LUCKIER I GET.

—Gary Player

Each practice session should vary according to your needs at that moment. One day, you may want to spend time on your full swing or putting, while another day, chip shots and bunker play might be your focus. Other times, you may feel like adding some creativity to the mix and figure out how to make the ball fly low or left or long. Every now and then, you may just need to get away from real life and lose yourself in the exhilaration and joy of letting the ball soar skyward, carrying your troubles away with it.

One of the unique features of golf is that you get to be your own coach. You decide what you need to work on, you personalize how you'll reinforce those ideas, and you design the practice sessions that will focus on what you want to improve. Have some fun with the time you're on the range. Divide your practice into three different approaches:

Repetition

Practice the motion repeatedly to learn the moves you want to make. As a motion becomes more automatic, you're free to *not* have to think about it anymore. In other words, you're really practicing to forget!

Creativity

Experiment with a variety of moves until you find the stroke you like. If you are hooking it, try some slice moves to straighten out the ball flight. Try creating shots with the same club that make the ball go high, low, left, or right. Use the same club to hit the ball to a target, halfway there, and then a quarter of the way there. Try this exercise with a wedge, a 7-iron and then a hybrid.

Imagery

Picture a golf hole on the course and play it right there on the range. Select the club for each shot you envision. Go through your mental and physical routines, and make the stroke that the picture calls for. You'll be practicing an invaluable skill to use on the course: allowing the stroke to be created from the picture in your mind.

FROM GAME PLAN TO GAME ON

Game plans provide a positive course of action for *what* and *how* you will think while you're playing the game. Don't make a plan that you can't control or bring to fruition, like "no bogeys today" or "I'm going to shoot below a certain number" just because it's the result you would like. Do make a plan that includes a small task you can easily repeat, like taking a breath before each shot or holding your finish.

The ability to stay focused on one thought is one of the most powerful assets of a strong mental game. It doesn't matter which task you choose for a particular round because every task will channel your thoughts where you want them to be. Training your brain to have only one thought is a way to practice and achieve the single-mindedness you'll need to play your best golf more often. When you are able to stay involved in a process using the task you've chosen for the round (that challenging yet simple assignment you can execute with every shot), your focus is on something you can control.

Once a skill no longer takes any added energy to perform and has become an established part of how you play, you're ready to practice the next step in training your golf mind. Be patient. It's up to you to keep the process simple. System overload won't get you where you want to be; it will actually hold you back. Don't overwhelm yourself by trying to practice more than one task at a time, because more often than not, the harder you try, the worse you get. You'll be able to go from the range to the course, from game plan to game on, each time you pick a plan you can carry out and stick to your process of actually doing it.

CHAPTER NINE

THE POINT OF NO RETURN

THE END IS THE BEGINNING

Now that you've discovered *Point A*, you're at *Point A*. It is a major turning point in your golf journey and also a point of no return. You won't want to go back to endless practice hours on the road to nowhere or rounds filled with more frustration than fun. You're on the launch pad heading toward the success you've dreamed about. How far you travel with *Point A* thinking is up to you. Best of all, the sky is the limit to how far you can go and *Point A* is the rocket ship that will take you there.

Everyone can play this game! There's no perfect anything required to play golf because golf fits everyone perfectly. Golf is unique in so many ways but none more appealing than the fact that anyone can play this game.

"Golf is about as adaptable a sport as you can get," said Bob Buck, executive director of the Eastern Amputee Golf Association. "Just about anyone, regardless of ability level, can grab a set of golf clubs, head outside and in no time be hitting golf balls where no one will ever find them again."

There are golfers that are young and old, short and tall, big and little, some athletic and some not, but all are able to enjoy the challenge and rewards of playing the game. From toddlers (Tiger Woods was only two when he started) to teenagers to golden agers well into their nineties, golfers of all ages can be seen on driving ranges and courses all over the world. Golf is available to just about everyone everywhere. Golf truly is a one-size-fits-all sport.

There is no one and only swing,
>only your swing.

There is no perfect swing,
>only more or less efficient swings.

There is no exact way to play golf,
>everyone's game is unique.

The golf stroke is a natural motion unique to each person. Since there is no perfect swing, all you have to do is develop the one you already have. There's no need to try to copy any other player's stroke. That would be like trying to trace your own signature or copy someone else's. It's tedious and never an exact replica. Your swing is like your signature and you're the only one who can write it effortlessly, efficiently, and without conscious thought.

ZONE IN TO YOUR ZONE

We often hear golfers and other athletes talking about how they played in the zone. Have you ever wondered what this zone is or how to get there? Where is the door and what secret password do you need to access this mysterious place? It's not out there someplace where you have to look for it. It's in the Marvelous You waiting for you to tap into its tranquility and power. When you are so deeply immersed in what you are doing that there's nothing else in your mind competing for your attention, you are in the zone.

The zone is a place where focus, self-confidence, and trust rule above all else. The zone is where the Marvelous You exists, always ready to guide and glide you through every action to your highest possible performance level. There is no instruction or self-talk or trying in the zone.

The zone is truly a magical place where you experience the best of who you are. It's a thought-free paradise of efficiency and gracefulness. Athletes, surgeons, musicians, artists, actors, and countless others in all kinds of occupations and hobbies have all been there. Children play in the zone all the time. They are so engrossed in what they are doing that there is nothing but the game for them. Their attention is centered on playing the game and having fun.

Your mind is completely calm when you're in the zone. Everything feels effortless, and every move is natural, unforced, and spontaneous. You're thoroughly absorbed in what you're doing; completely unaware of what's happening outside of you. You are so deeply in the moment that time feels like it's moving in slow motion and often not at all. There is no past. There is no future. There are no distractions. There is no leaderboard. There is no score. You're at *Point A*.

Point A thinking allows you to play like a child—unencumbered by inhibitions and fears. It clears away the chaos. The negativity, anxiety, and expectations that often obscure the way into the zone don't exist at *Point A*. There is only here and now and the opportunity to let the Marvelous You zone into your zone.

JOURNAL YOUR JOURNEY

Journaling is the one tool that people from all walks of life find useful in their quest for improving their lives and their skills. It's a simple written reflection of valuable past experiences to increase and imbed the memory of those experiences so as to learn from them. If you're the kind of person who finds this to be an unappealing and onerous task, there's no need to read the following suggestions. They won't help you. Just skip it. However, if your interest is piqued, journaling can greatly improve how you manage *you* and your golf game.

Studies have shown that writing boosts your memory. Writing about a positive experience allows your brain to relive it, reinforcing self-confidence and self-esteem. Writing about an unwanted experience helps you to understand it more and let it go. Your reflections on the events of the round and how you reacted to them will be the building blocks that improve your game and your scores.

Use these questions to guide your reflections:
What was my game plan?
Did I stick to my game plan?
What did I do well?
What would I change if I could?
What were my thoughts before a missed shot?
What *Point A* tool helped me?
What do I want to work on?

Recalling your observations and taking the time to write them in a journal after the round will help you devise a positive and purposeful plan for what you want to practice or incorporate into your next round. And with no additional effort, there's a terrific added bonus. Should you forget anything, it's all where you can find it, ready for you to revisit and reflect upon for years to come.

NEVER, NEVER, NEVER GIVE UP

Birdies happen. Bogies happen. Golf isn't predictable, and there is no script. Whether you open your round with an eight or end it with one, it's still the same eight, and scoring one doesn't grant you immunity from scoring another and another, nor are you guaranteed that making that unfortunate blunder will reward you with a birdie.

Carly, a 14-handicapper who was playing in the Seniors' Trophy Tournament of her small golf organization, had been playing *Point A* golf for just over a year. Coming into the par-4 9th hole, she had a score of 39 including the one-shot penalty for landing in the water hazard on the 5th hole. Her tee shot ricocheted off a rock outcropping on the right side of the fairway and landed under a tree next to a root. She punched out to the fairway and played the next shot and each shot after it from *Point A*. Carly forgot about the past (using the image of a brick wall) and did not worry about the future (using the idea of scissors to cut the emotional ties to the outcome). She made an 8 on the hole and strode quietly and calmly to the 10th tee.

IF YOU ARE GOING THROUGH HELL, KEEP GOING.
—Winston Churchill

Carly was determined to stay in her process as she prepared to hit her drive. Her plan was to be at *Point A* for every shot. She played a solid back nine very much within the range of her abilities. She wasn't carrying the weight of any thoughts about her score on the front nine, so she wasn't distracted by feelings of embarrassment, disappointment, defeat, or anger.

Going into the final holes, she had carded three pars, four bogeys, and a double bogey, giving her a score of 40 for eight holes on the back nine. She stood on the eighteenth tee, a par-3 over water, totally unaware of her score. Her next shot would be just another shot from *Point A*: no pressure, no worries, and no expectations. A confident, solid stroke sent the ball soaring high, finding its way to the green and leaving her an uphill left-to-right curling putt to the hole.

She casually repaired a pitch mark in her line, returned to the ball, took her stance, and set the ball in motion. Time seemed to stand still. She watched as the ball rolled smoothly over the restored flat surface toward the left rim of the cup, and as if it had been pulled uphill by some magical magnetic force, it tracked straight into the bottom of the cup. The glorious kerplunkity, gurgily sound reverberated in her ears. The birdie 2 gave her a 42 on the back nine, bringing her total numbers on the scorecard to an 89 for the round.

Her positive outlook remained intact no matter where the ball was or what her score was. She forgot all about the quadruple bogey on the 9th hole. She didn't think about averaging the 8 down with a birdie or pressuring herself into trying to do something that was out of her control. She played the back nine unperturbed by her score because she was committed to her plan to play each shot from *Point A* ... and she did. She never gave up, and much to her surprise and delight, she beat the field and won by one stroke.

A GOOD STROKE AND A STROKE OF GOOD LUCK

Once a golf ball leaves the clubhead, there's simply no telling exactly where it will land or ultimately come to rest. A capricious bounce on the cart path can add fifty yards, plop the ball into a pond, or drop it five inches from the flagstick. Where the ball ends up is about as unpredictable as tomorrow's headlines, and as fate would have it, in golf as in life, no one knows what will happen next.

In the final round of the 2013 President's Cup at Muirfield Village in Columbus, Ohio, Phil Mickelson experienced both good and bad luck in one shot. He hit a drive that landed in the rough on a steep incline way to the right of the fairway. From that awkward downhill lie, he visualized the next shot going over the water and onto the green. When he made the shot, the ball hit a tree slightly right of the intended line of flight—bad luck—and made a sharp left turn into the water—more bad luck. Next, it miraculously skipped from the surface of the water onto solid ground and landed safely a few feet from the water's edge—very good luck!

Both good and bad luck are built into the nature of the game, and even if it doesn't always appear that way, both good and bad luck fall equally on the golf course. When you accept this fact, you are less frustrated, kinder to yourself, and able to stay more positive about your next shot.

If you hate bunker shots, it's lucky for you when your ball lands on the rake in the bunker and then pops onto the grass. It's lucky for your opponent but not so lucky for you when his/her skulled chip shot sends the ball racing across the green only to be stopped by the pin and drop into the hole. It has been said that there isn't a shot on the golf course that doesn't please somebody!

THE GLASS EYE

Emily and Mike spent most vacations traveling to golf destinations, happily working their way down their bucket list of dream venues. Their most memorable story comes from a round on the King's Course in Gleneagles, Scotland, where they experienced the highs and lows of the game through the insightful commentary offered by their inimitable caddies. They had been told by a friend who lived near Gleneagles that they must look up a particular caddie known to all as "The Captain." Luckily, he was available and did caddie for Mike. Angus, his deadpan-faced friend, caddied for Emily.

The Captain, with his piercing one-liners shared in his very strong Scottish brogue at the most opportune moments, was indeed an unforgettable character. His witty asides punctuated the round as often as the fickle Scottish weather changed from sun to showers and back again. The story that unfolded became a classic that was told at every gathering of their golf-loving friends.

Both players hit good shots off the first tee. As they walked down the fairway, the friendly banter between caddies and players set a jovial tone for what was to become a very memorable round. The sun was shining when they began the round but was soon darting in and out of the clouds that were so close to the earth they seemed near enough to reach up and touch. Closing the umbrella for the third time, the Captain said, "Aye. Scotland. It's a *grrreat* place to live. We've got everything here we need…except a *rrroof*!" Everyone laughed as the jovial group made their way to the next tee and to everyone's delight, the one-liner gems and informative commentary from their very witty star caddie continued throughout the round.

Mike hit his career drive off the tee of the 455-yard par-5 6th hole. It was a solid, very long beauty that split the fairway with surgical precision. He followed that spectacular shot with a 3-wood that dropped the ball just short of the front of the green. It took several hops and rolled as if on some predestined path directly toward the hole, coming to rest about six feet from the cup. The opportunity for an eagle three put a grin on his face and a bounce in his step. No one spoke as they walked toward the green.

They marked the balls on the green, and everyone carefully and quietly moved out of Mike's line of sight and stood as still as statues while he studied the line from the ball to the hole and the hole to the ball. There was an opinion or two from the Captain about direction and pace as he held the flag tight to the flagstick so it too would be silent.

Mike set up to the ball. He looked at the line, looked at the ball, looked at the line again, looked at the ball again, and took the putter back. The sound of metal making solid contact with the ball rang out loud and clear. Time stood still. Everyone watched as the ball slowly and steadily inched its way toward the hole and rolled over the left edge of the cup. All eyes were riveted on the ball, now motionless and sitting two inches past the hole.

Everyone felt the disappointment. No one uttered a word as every head bowed with compassion and empathy. After a respectful pause, the caddies lifted the bags onto their shoulders and led the solemn procession slowly off the green. As they approached the next tee, the Captain looked up at Mike and offered the following words of consolation: "Aye, golf. 'Tis a *gemme* tha' can *brrring* a tear to a glass eye."

Everyone stopped walking, the world stopped spinning, and they nervously looked from one to another. Within seconds, a burst of uproarious laughter united the jovial group, and they began to walk to the 7th tee. With *Point A* thinking, the missed putt is a thing of the past until it's recounted in the tale that will be told in the grill room after the round. The only shot of interest now is on the 7th tee, at *Point A*.

GO PLAY!

Golf is a game like no other. You can play for the sheer joy of it, the inherent beauty in it, the excitement of the competition, the endless challenges it offers, or all of it combined. Now that you've reached the end of this book you're at the beginning of a new way to think about golf. You're ready to take your game from the printed page to the range and the course. It's time to weave the common sense of *Point A* into what you think, how you think, and when you think it.

Play from *Point A*.
> There is no past.
> There is no future.
> There is only here and now.

Play with a Process.
> Aware of who *you* are.
> Allow instead of try.
> Accept that each new shot is a new opportunity.

Play with Positivity.
> Visualize what you want.
> Trust that you can do it.
> Look for the good in every situation.

Golf truly is "a *gemme* tha' can *brring*" happiness, immeasurable satisfaction, stories that never lose their luster, and a lifelong journey of personal growth to everyone who plays it. You need only bring your clubs, your heart, and a *Point A* point of view... and that's the point!

So now that you've come to *Point A*,

You know it's where you want to stay.

With techniques of all kind,

Far out of your mind,

It's amazing how well you can play!

—B.T. ENOS AND VALERIE LAZAR

ACKNOWLEDGEMENTS

The first note of thanks must go to Susie Meyers: my golf instructor, dear friend, and partner in the creation of *Golf from Point A*. Her broad-based experience as a professional tour player, the coach of PGA champions, and a highly respected instructor to golfers of every skill level has proven the wide range of success that's achievable with *Point A* thinking. She leaves an imprint of her passion for the game with every student she touches. It's no coincidence that in the time since we reconnected in 2011 and began this project—after more than twenty years from one lesson to the next—my golf game continues to improve every time I play. Our collaboration is an amalgam of the ideas we shared and developed and, most importantly, how to make them accessible and beneficial to every golfer of every skill level.

I am grateful beyond measure to my dear friends and family for their encouragement during the past four years.

Without the untiring support of my husband, Ken, this book could not have been written. He and I have been holding each other's hands and memories for over fifty years—a span that has yielded two children, five grandchildren, two dogs, and three holes-in-one.

My daughter, Emily, was my confidant and advisor on all things creative and computer related. My son, Michael, and daughter-in-law, Lauren, were my golf-savvy listeners with spot-on feedback. My brother, David Niles, and Emmora Irwin were a significant part of *Point A* from the very beginning. The developmental stages, enlivened by spirited discussions and delicious dinners, will long be remembered. David's expertise and guidance throughout the entire process and his design for the book cover and logo were invaluable. My sister, Vicky—who, like my brother, has never picked up a golf club and probably never will—offered the practical perspective of a non-golfer on the clarity of the text. My father, with his two-finger prowess on a 1952 Smith Corona and skilled storytelling, taught me that words are sparkling jewels that can glow forever. My mother, who gifted me with music and whose dream to become a teacher was realized through me, showed me by example that giving up is never an option.

My friends Alanna Berger, Ellen Hodor, Rita and Michael Forrester, and Michelle and Tony Pisacano gave generously of their time to proofread the early manuscripts and serve as a test laboratory for its ideas. They embraced *Golf from Point A* and verified that it truly is a game changer.

Ken has often said, "You can lead a normal life, or you can play golf—take your pick." I pick golf.

VL

A special thanks to Brittany Benvenuto, who has read and listened to every piece of this book in its making; to Sue Pregartner, for always giving me sound advice and a kick in the pants when needed; and to Erich and Kelly Kuhlman, for their forever friendship and support. The members of the Ventana Canyon Golf and Racquet Club have believed in me and entrusted me with their golf games, and the staff has backed me and encouraged me for over twenty years.

David Niles and Emmora Irwin have been instrumental from the inception of this book and have added knowledge and creative skills to all parts of our book, including the cover and our logo. I am grateful for the work Duane Bernard did with the manuscript and his wife, Christa Johnson, who has been my friend and sounding block for years. Thanks go to Malinda Magel, who has contributed to the promotion and ideas to move the book forward, and Tom Conran, for helping me get into the twenty-first century.

A simple thank you to this great game of golf that has enhanced my life in so many ways. I have had special golf instructors, mentors, and coaches, like Michael Hebron and Jack Conrad, who have guided and inspired me. My mother and father introduced me to the game, and my brother motivated me from the very beginning. My sister has been my hero and someone I could always count on. I feel so fortunate to have my husband, Dan, and our two children, Carly and Christopher, as my biggest fans. They have uplifted me throughout this process and been my foundation to allow me to do what I love.

SM

ABOUT THE AUTHORS

From camp counselor to President of the Women's Metropolitan Golf Association, for as long as I can remember I have always been interested in learning and teaching. My background in education and the wide variety of positions I've held that required organizational and leadership skills gave me the life experiences I needed to be able to structure the material in Golf From *Point A* into a simple, and logical format.

I graduated from Hunter College with a BA in Sociology, earned my New York State certification in elementary education, and immediately began my formal teaching career. *Point A* simplicity was apparent in my earliest lesson plans. To enrich the required curriculum, I created a syllabus that integrated America's great folk songs into the study of American history, allowing the melodies and descriptive lyrics to tell the stories of the people and their times. My students discovered that learning important facts, names, and dates through music could be as easy as singing the alphabet song. Instinctually, I had removed the onerous task of trying to learn by rote in the same way that *Golf from Point A* removes the need to remember an overload of isolated instructions while trying to swing a golf club.

Speaking of swinging a club, somewhere in the mid-1980s, I discovered golf. I had always enjoyed sports, and although I was an avid tennis player at the time, I eagerly retired my racquet in exchange for a set of golf clubs the moment that first good shot flew effortlessly off the clubface. I was instantly hooked on the game and found myself wanting to play or practice as often as I could. In 1987, I became a member of the Women's Metropolitan Golf Association and in 1989 I was invited to join the Women's Tri-County Golf Association. Both venues offered friendly competition at some of the most sought-after golf courses in the New York metropolitan area.

I was elected to the boards of both Associations. During my eight-year tenure on the board of the Women's Met, I served as recording secretary, vice president (1993–1994), and president (1995–1996). I represented the organization at four French–American Challenge Competitions (Metropolitan Golf Association/Women's Metropolitan Golf Association vs. Ligue de Paris) as the Women's team captain: 1992 at St. Germain, France;

1994 at St. Cloud, France; 1995 at the Creek Club, Locust Valley, NY; and 1996 at the Racing Club/La Boulie, France.

While a member of the Carnegie Club at Skibo Castle in Dornoch, Scotland, I played on the winning teams in the Haskells Competition against Royal Dornoch and the Spirit Kettle Competition against Nairn. I have been the Women's club champion or runner-up for many years at two New York metropolitan-area country clubs. Most recently, I won the Women's Tri-County Super Senior and Legends Tournaments—proof positive that playing golf, like vintage wine, can improve with age.

Golf has been the mainspring of many of my dearest friends and a raison d'être for travels both near and far. My love for this captivating and challenging game has taken me to places I could never have imagined—not the least of which is the authorship of this book.

VALERIE LAZAR
RYE, NEW YORK

My journey in the game of golf up to the publication of this book began when I was fourteen. That is when I picked up a golf club for the first time. I instantly fell in love with the game. At first, like others, I wasn't very good, but I still remember the day during that first year of playing that I made a statement to myself: "I will play on the LPGA Tour."

Ten years later, that dream came true. It didn't happen because I was a great ball striker but because I was learning to play golf from what I now call *Point A* to *Point A*. Along with a strong mental game, I had developed a great short game and a way of thinking that was positive as I paid attention to what was working and never to what was not.

I played golf at the University of Arizona, where I earned All American status. Then, I joined the ranks of many young golfers who were playing mini tour golf to gain experience and to enhance the skills needed to play on the LPGA Tour. These experiences also added to the development of the concepts of *Point A* golf listed here.

During this mini tour stage and while playing on the LPGA Tour, I never saw my swing on video. I learned to play professionally through experience and instruction given with broad concepts, not minute details. On the mini tour, I learned to win and honed my playing skills so that I could stand over a ball and not have to think about the mechanics to make my stroke.

I qualified for the LPGA Tour in 1984, and the next three years spent there were like getting my master's degree. It was the hard work and difficult experiences that helped me grow. I gained a deeper understanding of the baby steps of the process that would make a difference in reaching my goals. It wasn't the big leaps but the small tasks that I would master that helped form my game. I played in four US Opens and one LPGA Championship and was second on the money list for two years on the mini tour.

Once off the LPGA Tour I was given a life changing opportunity by Pete Donnelly to teach at Ridgeway Country Club in Westchester County, New York. Without Pete I may have never fallen in love with this side of golf. I had never thought of myself as a teacher; however, when I gave my first lesson, I instantly knew that I had found what I would do for the rest of my life. Being able to help people made me happy. I joined the PGA of America and began to educate myself. I wanted to grow and learn all I could and found myself very interested in the technique and details of how a golf swing worked. I traveled all over the country shadowing instructors and even studied *The Golfing Machine*. I was fortunate enough to work with Michael Hebron, Jim McLean, and Hank Haney, all professionals listed at one time in the top five in the world.

My career really changed during the next stage of my journey when I moved to Tucson, Arizona, and began teaching at the Ventana Canyon Golf and Racquet Club. This was when I met Jack Conrad, a lifetime PGA professional who had played on the PGA Tour when he was young. He was what is often referred to as an "old time" professional. Jack was a philosopher, and his philosophy resonated with me immediately because he was putting into words things I had experienced as a player. His ideas also changed how I perceived the golf stroke and how I personally made my golf stroke. Things became much simpler and more powerful. He helped me learn to communicate to my students that there was a way to think about golf that was more than just the technique of the golf stroke. All this helped me see the game more clearly and was instrumental in the development of *GOLF from Point A*.

Researching and studying with Michael Hebron, a PGA Hall of Fame instructor, about how people learn and what is going on in the brain helped me to structure my teachings to get people on a simpler and more successful path to reaching their goals. Michael afforded me the opportunity to speak with golf professionals from all over the world, like Chile, India, Ireland, and England. Michael has had a profound influence on who I am today and is a big part of the essence of *GOLF from Point A*.

Every student that has stood in front of me has helped me grow as a teacher and a coach. Having Michael Thompson walk into my life when he was fourteen years old and coaching him to the PGA Tour and his first win was a blessing. It was an honor to work with such a fine young man.

A few years ago, Derek Ernst showed up on my lesson tee as a rookie on the PGA Tour, and after spending two days working with the *Point A* philosophy, he went out and won his first Tour event three weeks later. Derek thanked me during his press conference. What a thrill to see these ideas put into action so quickly and so successfully.

These are the same ideas that many club golfers have thanked me for sharing with them over the years. When put into play, *Point A* golf is more about learning to change how one looks at playing golf than making detailed swing changes. With broad ideas, you can change what your golf ball is doing without thinking about every body part and how it moves. Using *Point A* thinking has given my students the clarity and courage to cast away expectations and do the best they possibly can at that moment in time to make their golf stroke. That is what I strive to do every day.

My family has been my inspiration and foundation. Dan, my husband, is a fine player who takes my advice only from listening to me help others. Teaching your husband is a bit dangerous! Our two children have helped me grow in so many ways. Coaching my son with suggestions based on *Point A* golf has been my biggest challenge and greatest reward. Christopher now plays golf at Stanford University. Carly is going to Arizona State University and will be a special needs preschool teacher. Her heart and soul is about helping young people develop the skills to be the best that they can be.

SUSIE MEYERS
TUCSON, ARIZONA

WORKS CITED

Buck, Bob. Executive Director, Eastern Amputee Golf
Association.

Crouse, Karen. "Out of the Pool, Phelps Finds the Water
at Medinah." *The New York Times*. September 25,
2012. Accessed April 01, 2016.

http://www.nytimes.com/2012/09/26/sports/golf/golfing-a
t-medinah-club-michael-phelps-feels-tug-of-water-
holes.html?_r=0.

Goose, Mother. "Humpty Dumpty sat on a wall." *Poetry
Foundation*. Accessed April 01, 2016. http://www.
poetryfoundation.org/.

Hoff, Benjamin. *The Tao of Pooh*. New York: Penguin
Books, 1982.

Kay, Emily. "Rory McIlroy Reveals British Open-winning
'trigger Words.'" SBNation.com. July 20, 2014.
Accessed April 06, 2016. http://www.sbnation.com/

golf/2014/7/20/5920683/rory-mcilroy-trigger-words-british-open-2014.

Piper, Watty, and Mabel C. Bragg. The Little Engine *That Could*. New York: Platt & Munk, 1961.

Seuss, Dr. *Oh, the Places You'll Go!* New York: Random House, 1990.

Printed in the USA
CPSIA information can be obtained
at www.ICGtesting.com
LVHW010956260823
756385LV00039B/760